THE
DYSLEXIC
EDGE

THE
DYSLEXIC
EDGE

JAMIE WALLER

WITH DR HELEN TAYLOR

First published in Great Britain in 2024 by
Love Yellow Limited, in partnership with Whitefox Publishing

www.wearewhitefox.com

ISBN 978-1-916797-42-0
Also available as an eBook ISBN 978-1-916797-43-7
and an audiobook ISBN 978-1-916797-46-8

Cover design by Love Yellow Limited
Adapted for print by Simon Levy Associates
Typeset by seagulls.net
Project management by Whitefox
Printed and bound by CPI Group (UK) Ltd, Croydon CR0 4YY

For the dyslexic thinkers who are having
a positive impact on the world

CONTENTS

FOREWORD

BY DR HELEN TAYLOR

I am delighted to be collaborating with Jamie on this book about the links between dyslexia and success. I've been researching in this area for twenty years and for most of that time, dyslexia has been viewed by academia as a dysfunction. My research aims to change those perceptions by explaining what dyslexic brains have evolved to do and why. By doing this, I aim to show the many benefits this way of thinking brings to individuals, to business and society in general. *The Dyslexic Edge* shares those aims.

We've known for a long time that there are high numbers of people with dyslexia who are successful in the field of entrepreneurship. This success is often attributed to particular strengths they are found to possess, such as strategic focus, resilience and delegation skills. However, within many fields including entrepreneurship, strengths are often explained as arising from adverse experiences.

For example, strengths in delegation identified in studies of dyslexic entrepreneurs have been interpreted as a 'coping strategy' developed because of the need to rely on other people to accomplish certain tasks they found challenging. Other studies have found that dyslexics excel in interpersonal communication, but this has been interpreted as a strategy to compensate for their lack of written skills. In fact, many of the positive traits associated with dyslexia are often framed in a similarly deficit-centric way.

This is not surprising given the current framing of dyslexia as a specific learning disability. Understandably, most research has tried to remediate educational challenges. Consequently, difficulties are traditionally the main focus. But mounting evidence from a number of areas suggests that we need a new approach and even a new field of research that seeks to also understand the flip side of dyslexia – that is, the *strengths* that emerge from this way of thinking, including why they exist and how they benefit society.

My own research has been uncovering evidence that, rather than a learning *disorder*, people with dyslexia have a learning *specialisation* that is critical to human prosperity.

I first started questioning the traditional deficit-centred approach because I didn't understand how someone could have a disorder with writing, a human-made technology that was invented relatively recently. Behaviourally modern humans have existed for at least 50,000 years, but writing, first invented around 5,000 years ago, has only been used widely in the last century. This questions the assumption that writing difficulty should be viewed as a 'deficit'. Indeed, writing is one of the few, if not only, cultural inventions where we equate difficulty with deficit.

Indeed, the difficulty that so many people have with reading and writing provides us with a tantalising clue about brain development. The ease with which people can learn and use this technology varies widely among us, suggesting that human brains process information differently. Identifying exactly what that cognitive difference is and why it exists has been a key focus of my research.

To figure out what that difference is, I initially looked for a common pattern linking the different behavioural strengths often associated with dyslexia. I found that they are all in some way related to learning through *exploration*, that is, the development of *new* knowledge, be that creating an original invention or strategy, or discovering some fundamental truth about the world.

When I examined the available cognitive psychology and neuroscience evidence, I found that the same emphasis on exploration was mirrored in how the brains of people with dyslexia process information. This is very exciting, since connecting research on dyslexia with neuroscience research on exploratory learning provides a bridge to understanding the brain differences that underlie dyslexic strengths. An exploratory specialisation would also explain why 'dyslexic thinking' is so important in business and society.

The evidence also shows that this talent for exploring comes at the expense of abilities in repetition or *exploitation* of *existing* knowledge. 'Exploitation of existing knowledge' is almost a summary of the focus

of all western school systems: copying from others, or books, and rote learning and memorising existing human knowledge. Exploiting existing knowledge is obviously very important, as it's a fast track to learning what has sometimes taken many generations to understand.
But learning in this way has major limitations. What if you want to improve things? Or what if your environment changes? Then you need to explore and create new knowledge, and this is where dyslexia's exploratory tendencies come to the fore.

Exploration and exploitation exist along a continuum from simply exploiting (e.g. copying an existing solution), to exploring just a little, to refining an invention or an idea, to a larger global search to arrive at a highly original solution. It's for this global end of exploratory learning that my research suggests people with dyslexia are specialised. But why would this specialisation exist? The answer lies deep in the human past.

Human evolution was shaped by dramatic climate variability. To adapt and survive our ancestors had to continually update their knowledge and behaviours. They had to be exceptional at exploring globally to create big-picture solutions, developing them locally to refine them and consolidating useful knowledge. But an individual human brain is limited in its capacity. The theory of 'Complementary Cognition' proposes that humans evolved to specialise individually in different but complementary aspects of this knowledge creation process. Collaboration made us exceptional at co-creating the knowledge we needed to adapt and survive.

Just like human groups in the past, organisations also need to balance this exploration–exploitation trade-off in order to adapt and prosper. Exploration in the world of business is often captured by terms like risk-taking, experimentation, play, flexibility, discovery and innovation. Exploitation, on the other hand, encompasses terms like refinement, choice, production, efficiency, implementation and execution. Maintaining a balance between exploration and exploitation is a primary factor in any firm's survival and prosperity. Indeed, it's been linked to higher sales growth, innovation and market valuation.

In the entrepreneurial stage of a business, or when businesses need to adapt to change, exploration is particularly important. This is likely why dyslexics are so over-represented among entrepreneurs.

As we'll see in the interviews in this book, people with dyslexia excel where there's uncertainty and complexity. They explore in their imagination to design novel solutions, explore in time to envision new possibilities and bring together teams, aligning them to achieve a common vision. My research suggests that people with dyslexia succeed in business leadership because their brains are suited to it.

The interviewees demonstrate so clearly how dyslexic thinking has driven their success, but these people may be the lucky few who have managed to reach their potential. Their stories also highlight how the current education system seems to be failing people with dyslexia. As a result, society may be losing thousands upon thousands of inventive, insightful and visionary individuals who have the potential to excel in entrepreneurship, make great discoveries in science and help us adapt to the enormous sustainability challenges that we now face. With this book, we are working to rewrite the narrative. My hope is that in the future, people with dyslexia will no longer be sidelined by society and classified as having a learning disability, but will instead be recognised for their strengths in global exploration.

Dr Helen Taylor

INTRODUCTION

The idea to write this book came from one of the most famous dyslexics on the planet, Sir Richard Branson. I was spending time at his home on Necker Island, and while we were on a bike ride our conversation turned to dyslexia. We're both dyslexic and both have hyperactive brains; the conversation was expansive and soon turned to sleep and the link between dyslexia and sleep disorders. I wondered if dyslexia was also the reason we were drawn to become entrepreneurs. Later that day, Richard gave me some notes scribbled on a torn piece of paper (apparently, Sir Richard often uses bits of scrap paper to deliver messages) with advice and wisdom on sleeping.

This got me thinking – how many entrepreneurs have dyslexia, and what else might we have in common? I took some time in the Caribbean sun and started researching potential links. The connections I found between dyslexia, entrepreneurship and financial success were staggering. One statistic showed that 40 per cent of self-made millionaires are dyslexic, another that 35 per cent have dyslexia.* That's astonishing when you consider that people with dyslexia comprise less than 15 per cent of

---

* Logan, J. (2009). 'Dyslexic entrepreneurs: The incidence; their coping strategies and their business skills'. *Dyslexia*, 15(4), 328–346.

the population. Far from being a disadvantage, when it comes to success, dyslexia appears to be something of a superpower. And yet, most people still see it as a disability.

Dyslexia is a specific learning disability. The term dyslexia refers to a cluster of symptoms that result in people having difficulties with specific language skills, particularly reading.

Unsurprisingly, most of us with dyslexia don't do well at school. In fact, many of us have painful memories of being sent to the back of the class because the teachers, as well as the other kids, thought we were thick. For me, that led to bullying, which had a big impact on my self-confidence as a child.

Even though it's been decades since I left school, dyslexia is still associated with having a low IQ. Thankfully, the latest research is flipping old assumptions on their head. Instead of fixating on what dyslexic brains can't do, academics like Dr Helen Taylor are now questioning what dyslexic brains are built to do.

Researchers, practitioners and charities have been observing for decades that people with dyslexia seem to excel in particular realms of mechanical and visual-spatial ability, as well as in creating and communicating insightful or original ideas. Research in entrepreneurship suggests we excel in areas such as big-picture thinking and strategic focus, delegation and risk-taking, and that we're more willing to challenge the status quo. No wonder so many of us have found success in business.

Before researching this book, I had often wondered if I started my own businesses because it was the only option for someone who left school without any qualifications. But the more I spoke to other dyslexics and academics who specialise in this field, the more I realised that there is something about how the dyslexic brain works that lends itself to entrepreneurship. As someone with a brain that never switches off – a widespread trait, as we'll see – I wondered if it was possible to teach anyone to think like someone with dyslexia? What if I could show people *without* dyslexia how to harness the benefits of dyslexic thinking? If I could, it would have the power to transform people and create new opportunities.

But that wasn't my only motivation for this book. I was also inspired after two associates asked for my advice to help their children who were facing the challenges of living with dyslexia. Harry is eleven and went to the kind of small village school that many parents would want their children to attend. But even with small class sizes, teachers missed his dyslexia.

His dad told me they were just advised that he had problems reading, and it was only when Harry moved school aged nine that he got a diagnosis and the help needed. If he hadn't moved school, who knows what would have happened.

Harry now gets help, but it means he is taken out of class for one-to-one tutoring each day. Like any other eleven-year-old boy, Harry just wants to be like his mates and his dyslexia is making him feel unique for the wrong reasons.

This has led to him worrying, not sleeping and stressing about his friends and relationships.

Terry's* story is even more heart-rending. His mum told me that despite being very astute and exceptionally good at maths, he was refused entry to several schools as they were unable to deal with his severe dyslexia. Consequently, he took an overdose and has been self-harming. While listening to Harry's and Terry's parents, I thought about the positive impact dyslexia intervention could have on them *and* society.

To demonstrate what dyslexic thinking can offer the world, I've teamed up with Dr Helen Taylor, a respected academic who specialises in understanding the cognitive strengths of dyslexia, to look at why so many dyslexics succeed. Her theory is that dyslexia is not a disorder, but rather a difference that has allowed human groups to prosper. I've also sat down and interviewed thirteen other successful dyslexic thinkers – some of them famous, some billionaires and some of them nearer the start of their journeys – to look at the impact dyslexia has had on them. Through their real-life stories, I aim to demonstrate the value of dyslexic thinking.

For those with dyslexia, this book aims to give you confidence to embrace your learning difference and use your unique talents to think differently and succeed. For those without dyslexia, this book will share the dyslexic thinking skills that can lead to success. At the end of

---

* Terry's name has been changed for privacy reasons.

each chapter, we present the benefits of dyslexic thinking by giving practical tips that anyone can implement. And for governments worldwide, this book should focus your attention on early dyslexia intervention to harness substantial social and economic benefits.

I'm in my forties now, and like many people of my generation, I didn't hear the word dyslexia during my childhood. It wouldn't have been until my late twenties that I heard about it for the first time. However, I was too busy running my business by then to confirm my suspicion that it probably applied to me. And if I'm honest, there would have been a part of me that didn't want the label, because in the back of my mind Dyslexic = Thick.

Meeting my now wife, Madeleine, in my thirties made me question the role dyslexia had played in my life. Like me, Madeleine is also dyslexic, but unlike me, she went to an excellent school that intervened and gave her support before going on to university to gain impressive grades. Her educational attainment was so unlike the stereotype I had of dyslexia that I had to reassess my views about it.

Being dyslexic does not stop when you leave school, of course. Not a single day passes when I don't have to make some accommodation, whether that's avoiding being in a situation where I will have to read anything out loud, or taking about four times as long to read a document than anyone else.

Even though I now see dyslexia as an advantage, it still has the power to make me feel like a schoolboy who's being picked on by the teachers. It can render me ashamed and embarrassed, like the time I first met Madeleine's family. It was at a party for her father's retirement, and everyone had written down a memory or anecdote about him and put their piece of paper in a hat. We then drew them at random to read out. If you have dyslexia yourself, you can probably already feel my anxiety.

I picked up this piece of paper, stood up, and I just wanted the floor to open and swallow me. The right thing to have done would have been to say, 'I don't know what this says', but I didn't. I attempted it. I'd only been dating Madeleine for a few months and wanted her family to like me, and I was too embarrassed to not just read it out loud.

I can't remember the exact story, but it involved a praying mantis on a holiday in France. I'm not even sure that I'd heard of a praying mantis before. If I had, I'd never said it out loud, but I attempted to read it anyway. The whole table started laughing. One of the guests said, 'Oh, Jamie, you ruined the story.' She then corrected me, and I was mortified. I still want the floor to open and swallow me up just remembering it. This demonstrates the issues people with dyslexia navigate even as we get older. The public perception is that dyslexia is something that affects kids. I know that dyslexia can be a superpower when it comes to careers, but it can also be an Achilles heel. Even as a successful adult, there are moments when your dyslexia feels like someone walking up behind you and smashing you in the head.

However, as time has passed, all the contributors in this book have developed some coping mechanisms, which means incidents like the one above are few and far between. By sharing these techniques, I hope many more dyslexic people will reap the benefits and find success. And by showing everyone how to think a little differently, I hope to bring the benefits of dyslexic thinking to everyone. I want dyslexia to be embraced and viewed as a learning difference, not a difficulty, in schools, at home, in the workplace and by governments around the world.

Oh, and I should take this opportunity to point out that I don't often cycle with Sir Richard Branson. In fact, it was the first time I had met him, and I feel very blessed to have had that opportunity and that our conversation led to this book.

CHAPTER 1

CLIFF WEITZMAN – THE DYSLEXIC TECHIE

BUSINESS: FOUNDER OF SPEECHIFY
QUALIFICATIONS: DEGREE

What's 4,342 divided by sixteen? Now divide that by twelve. This is Cliff Weitzman's brilliant illustration of the computational load a dyslexic brain takes on when it tries to read a paragraph like this one. Each letter, each word needs to be calibrated and checked: he can do the mental arithmetic, but it takes time. Despite this, he claims to have read 200 books in the past year thanks to his own invention, the text-to-speech service Speechify. The business is now one of the hottest tech brands in the world of dyslexia. To meet Cliff now – not yet thirty, energetic, enthusiastic and so fit he can perform backflips – it's hard to imagine he ever struggled with anything.

'My teachers thought that I was slow, and my parents thought I was lazy. I couldn't figure out how to spell my last name or how to read the animal names in a children's book. I'd go to the library and sit in the children's section with all the soft toys and look at books that were really too young for me. Every day the librarian would wake me up because I had fallen asleep. I just found reading too boring.'

Cliff spent his early childhood in Israel and when his brother came along – Cliff is the oldest of five extremely accomplished siblings – and quickly surpassed his reading ability, it made Cliff want to read even more. His parents wanted him to enjoy books so much that his dad incentivised him: for every half hour spent reading, Cliff was rewarded with a half-hour bike ride with his dad. Those bike rides were so precious to him, but even though he was very motivated, he still couldn't read. However, Cliff could do something else: he could memorise.

'I was very competitive with my brother and we got paid a shekel – about a dollar fifty – for every book we read, so I found ways of getting the money. I asked my sister if she would read her book out loud and remembered every word.'

At this point in our conversation, Cliff recites entire passages of a kids' book about a turtle: everything he learned is still filed away and easily retrievable in his remarkably efficient brain. Cliff's mum did a lot of research about why, despite his obvious intelligence, her son was struggling to read and she got him tested for dyslexia when he was about nine.

'And lo and behold, I had dyslexia. To me, it was extremely relieving. I was like, wow, now I have a place to hang my hat. I never, ever grew up with the concept of dyslexia being a negative thing. Interestingly, I'm sure my grandmother was also dyslexic. No question. She grew up in Iran and moved to Israel when she was sixteen, which is when she had her first child. Her role in life was not a particularly academic one, so dyslexia was not particularly impactful on her.'

This is a great illustration of the point Dr Helen Taylor has made that changes in society – kids staying in school for longer, the decline of manual labouring jobs – mean current generations suffer from something previous generations didn't even know they had.

'When I was about twelve, I finally finished a book. It was a really interesting story, and I so didn't want to stop. My dad came in to tell me to go to sleep, but he saw that I was reading so he let me stay up. I remember crying because I was so happy that I actually finished a book. My dad had done a really good job of telling me how amazing books are and what a joy it is to read. I had thought that would be something I would never have access to and I was so happy, because if I read that book, it meant I would likely read others.'

However, just a couple of months later, his family moved from Israel to the US and Cliff had to learn a new language. It would be a long time before he read another book.

As a kid, Cliff had loved the Harry Potter novels so much that he made his father record an audio version in his native Hebrew. When the Weitzmans arrived in California, Cliff's primary tool for learning English was listening to the audio versions of J.K. Rowling's series.

'I knew the story really well, so I picked up a lot. And then I found Percy Jackson and *Game of Thrones* and *Atlas Shrugged*. In the beginning, I used to listen at like 0.75 speed and then one times, then 1.25 and then two times and then three times. I just got really fast at listening.'

One of the things that's become so clear researching for this book is that we all learn in different ways. Dyslexics struggle to comprehend written information, but like Cliff I've also realised that I learn – and, crucially, retain – information really well through listening. I know other people fall asleep to audiobooks, but to people like Cliff and me it's stimulating: audio learning is a game changer. Cliff's memory is also audio-based.

'I have a few phone numbers memorised from my childhood in Israel, and I remember them in Hebrew, not in English: I don't remember the number, but the *sounds* of the numbers. If I listen to a song three times, I'll have the entire song memorised. I probably have every single word from *Hamilton* the musical memorised. If you give me a word from *Hamilton* on its own, it would take me some time to place it, but I could tell you immediately where it is from in the play if you sang the word.'

At his new school, Cliff showed promise in maths, but wasn't able to move to the advanced class because he struggled to understand the questions. Once they were explained to him, he could come up with the answers easily. 'I could understand why language would be a barrier to learning geography or history, but math? Come on!'

Dyslexics face barriers like this every day: if we need to read a form to apply for a loan, or benefits, or read a travel review to book the right holiday, our struggles with reading mean we're always at a disadvantage.

One of the ways Cliff coped at school was to organise study groups with his classmates.

'Back then, my handwriting was completely illegible. I would write letters on top of each other, different sizes, no spaces between letters. I would spell the word "squirrel" with twelve letters. I convinced friends to come study with me and we would read the chapter together, but realistically, they would read out the chapter. In exchange, I would explain anything that they wouldn't catch, or I would organise the notes.'

In English, where he was in the bottom class, Cliff had a strict teacher who wanted written summaries of the books he assigned his students. Cliff found an audiobook of one of the titles on a computer in the library and asked if he could give an oral summary instead. The teacher let him arrive fifteen minutes early to give his speech, and through the course of the year Cliff became one of the best-performing kids in the class.

Cliff subsequently looked for an audio version of a chemistry textbook and when he couldn't find one, he and his brother Tyler cracked the digital rights management system on their Kindle and loaded a digital version of the book onto a computer. A basic text-to-speech application then read it out to them. 'I realised that there were a lot of PDFs that I was going to have to read, none of which had audiobooks. So I started hacking together this text-to-speech system that would read out PDFs.'

Eventually, this would become Speechify. In theory, technology should have also helped with Cliff's spelling but when he got that red squiggle under a word, he would right click for the options but couldn't tell which one to pick. It wasn't until he got a bit older and wanted to impress girls, he finally had the motivation to find out. 'It's a more expensive mistake to misspell a word when you're texting a girl than it is to misspell it in an essay. I was probably nineteen when I finally knew the difference between "to", "too" and "two".'

Despite his dyslexia, Cliff had an abundance of confidence, even from a young age. He puts his robust ego down to having two parents who showed him unconditional love. That confidence enabled him to start his first business venture while he was still at school. He negotiated discounts with local retailers and then sold coupon codes to his classmates. Not the typical business run by a high schooler. 'I thought it was very normal economics. You go and create a bulk discount and you sell the arbitrage you achieved. The most challenging part was walking into a store and asking the manager for a discount.'

Another teenage venture involved patenting a pressurised cannon that could shoot fire-retardant blankets over entire houses.

Cliff's formal dyslexia diagnosis meant he was allowed more time to take exams. Some of the other kids, and indeed some of his teachers, thought that gave him an unfair advantage. Thankfully, he was more than able to stand up for himself.

'I'd be like, excuse me, it's actually protected by California law. You're not allowed to discriminate against someone for learning disabilities. And if necessary I'd write a letter to the principal. I take 110 per cent responsibility for my learning, to the extent that school is a tool that I use to learn. School is not happening to me. I am happening to the school. I will find the book that I need. I will find the resource that I need. I will find the teacher that I need. I will switch to another school if I need to. I don't think it is an injustice that I have dyslexia, and I don't expect a teacher to go out of their way to accommodate me. It's very nice if they do, but I don't need them to. What they may not do is stand in my way of fixing the problem for myself.'

When it came to college, Cliff had lived in the US long enough to know what a difference getting into the right school could make to your life chances.

'It's a passport to wherever you want to go, but I realised that they're so oversubscribed it's almost a lottery. So how do you improve your odds of winning the lottery? You brute-force it. Instead of applying to eight colleges, which is typical, I applied to twenty-six schools.'

It's such a brilliant example of the power of thinking differently. In the end, Cliff got several offers and elected to study renewable energy engineering at Brown University. He chose the subject because he thought it was the field that would have the greatest impact on humanity for the subsequent fifty years. While that sounds like straightforward logical thinking, what he did when he got to Brown was counter-intuitive. When he discovered that he loved studying the economics module, he stopped taking those classes.

'Economics was something I really enjoyed and it came to me very intuitively. It was a waste to keep studying it because I knew I would read economics books for fun. I switched to computer science, which I was very bad at, because I knew that I would not pick up computer science on my own.'

During this time, his brother Tyler developed over forty apps for the iPhone and Cliff was instrumental in marketing them. He liked how quickly you could create a product and get it to market, especially compared to the years of research and development needed in the renewable energy sector. Fuelled by impatience – a common trait among dyslexics – Cliff joined hackathons, where he would help develop and build something over the course of a weekend.

'There might be thirty, forty or 400 people, typically computer science students, and there's a competition to see which team builds the best thing. I was on the winning team the first event I went to, and then I did another one, another one, and I won. It wasn't because I was the best computer scientist – in fact, at that point,

I did not know how to code. It was because I'd show up, jump on a table, do a backflip and tell people what I wanted to work on, and so people joined my team. I won because I would talk to more users than everybody else.'

And Cliff being Cliff, he kept finding ways – just like with his college applications – to tip the scales in his favour. 'There'd be an email list of attendees, so I'd look everybody up, find their LinkedIns, their GitHubs and their Facebooks. I'd look at their personal websites and identify who the three best designers were, who were the three best back-end guys, the best iOS developers. I'd message all those people beforehand, tell them what my idea was, and before we even showed up, I'd already have my group. The hackathons taught me that I needed to learn to code myself. In the same way that I knew that if I didn't learn to read, I wouldn't become the person I wanted to be, I knew that to become an entrepreneur I had to code because at the end of the hackathon, everyone went back to their own thing. To carry on developing, I had to code, hence enrolling in computer science classes.'

Of course coding is just another language, which means Cliff still had a disadvantage.

'At the time, IDEs, which is like Microsoft Word for writing code, didn't have spellcheck. I'd misspell a variable and the equivalent of writing 'cat' with a 'k' rather than a 'c' would break the program. I knew I had to get better at coding, so I'd go to the dining hall, find a bag of bread and turn it into eight peanut butter sandwiches, and then I would just sit with my peanut butter sandwiches in the computer science lab from like 9 a.m. till midnight, and then I'd do it again the next day. And after like one or two months of this, I got good enough to tell the difference between a bug that was because of a spelling mistake and a bug that was legitimate. And that's when I started to get good at computer science.'

I love this story. I think too many people have the impression that dyslexics are somehow gifted when it comes to tech. Cliff's story shows that anyone can get good at anything … so long as they work hard enough. Cliff eventually taught himself to develop apps and went on to take Brown's most advanced course in computer science, which he found very hard.

'I read something from Tiger Woods saying that golf is more of a mental game than a game of skill and I thought, well, I've got to work on my mental game. I got myself a little notebook and I wrote in it every night before I went to sleep and every morning when I woke up, "I'm good at computer science, I'm good at computer science."'

Throughout college, Cliff refined his text-to-speech application. 'The way that I use text-to-speech is if it's easy to understand, I listen very fast. If it's difficult to understand and very dense, I'll slow it down, but I couldn't listen to more than 500 words per minute because the computer wouldn't let me. I figured that if I typed the specific command into the terminal – a lot of this I learned from just googling – I could get it to speak faster. I could get it to 550 words per minute, but when I wanted to slow it down, I had to literally restart the computer. I needed to build something that would manually be able to speed up and slow down, so I wrote code for that, and then I started hiring people on Upwork, the online freelancer marketplace, to add to the software that I'd built.'

Delegation is a topic that will come up a lot in this book, but Cliff takes it to the next level. Inspired after reading – or rather listening to – Tim Ferriss's book *The 4-Hour Work Week*, Cliff outsourced as much work as he could.

In his senior year at Brown, Cliff started thinking about where his career would take him. He toyed with getting a job at somewhere like Google and played around with a couple of inventions that ranged from a 3D printed skateboard to underwear called Ball Armour that blocked radiation from reaching reproductive organs.

'By the time I graduated college, I'd built thirty-six different products – iPhone apps, websites, payment systems, etc. I'd won Stanford University's start-up pitch competition twice. I won MIT's start-up pitch competition twice also, and I came second or third in Harvard's. So I got really good at conveying my ideas, recruiting people to teams, leading those teams in hackathons, and I was technical enough.'

Unsure which direction to take, he wrote a thirty-page paper about his world views that he distilled down to twenty-eight principles. That led him to trying to do something that would specifically have helped his ten-year-old self back in that library back in Israel.

'Imagine if you could tell him that with text-to-speech he would be reading 100 plus books a year? Then I realised that text-to-speech would get ten times better. It made sense to work on this product because text-to-speech had really changed my life, and I was amazed that other people were not using it.'

Cliff's plan was to build the best text-to-speech product on the market. How he set about doing it is pretty incredible. First, he got a summer job teaching computer science that paid $8,000 a month. He negotiated free rent in the college dorm where he taught and then convinced two teachers at Brown to sponsor him as a visiting scholar. That gave him a student ID, let him attend classes and use the college facilities.

'I got to stay in the college environment and go to parties on the weekend, but after a workout every single morning I'd go to the dining hall, and I'd just code. I figured that if I worked for three months over the summer, I could pay for my food, my rent and miscellaneous costs for the year. It was an infinite burn rate that meant I could carry on doing it until something took off.'

While his own living expenses were covered by his summer job, Cliff had to find the money to pay the coders he hired on Upwork. And to do that, he found even more people on Upwork.

'I hired ten freelancers in the Philippines to find and apply to scholarships for me. I realised that if I applied to scholarships for people who were studying math, studying energy, were Jewish, from Marin County, had dyslexia, had ADHD, had a GPA [grade point average] above X, I was very likely to win. The challenge was not writing applications that would win, it was finding the right scholarships to apply for. I hired ten freelancers who would fill a Google Sheet, from 1 to 100, with relevant scholarships. And then I uploaded every essay I'd written to a shared Google Drive, and they would help me match the scholarship to the right essay. I'd go in and fix the essay and submit. I won a lot of money from applying to scholarships, and that's how I paid those freelancers.'

Early on, Cliff identified that there was a difference between Speechify as a product and Speechify as a company. While he had a clear picture of the former, he wasn't sure how the business might look.

'The moment where it really took off was at a conference in Florida called the International Dyslexia Association Conference. I snuck into the event, essentially made friends with people and at a certain point I got on the stage, did a backflip, plugged in my computer and demoed the product. Twelve school heads then offered to fly me out to their school to teach the kids how to use Speechify.'

For the next few months, he visited those schools and gave his presentation. 'Then I would sit in the back of the class and I would see how people used Speechify. And if it broke, I'd fix it. If it wasn't clear how to use it, I'd make it easier to use. If it didn't work on, like, a random Surface Pro, I'd figure out how to make that work.'

He honed the product, got better at search engine optimisation on the App Store and got really good at Facebook and Google ads.

'Around 2020, I started flying around to meet people who were running companies that were really good at customer acquisition. So that's the founders of Audible, of Grammarly, of Dollar Shave Club, of Goop, of Robinhood, of Netflix, of Lululemon. Every major company that was good at acquiring users, I analysed their Instagram, Twitter, Medium and I would just see how they bought ads. Then I was like, OK, well, who are the best people at creating content? So like Logan Paul, Mr Beast and Ali Abdaal. I would go and live in their house for one to three weeks at a time, see how they made content and got good at making content. That combination of being good at buying ads and making content was really powerful.'

And how did he get those introductions? He hired people on Upwork – of course – to find the contact details, LinkedIn and social media profiles for the CEOs. He then messaged them until they would jump on a Zoom with him. It's not too dissimilar to how I introduced myself to some of the interviewees in this book, including Cliff. He says he still sends five cold messages almost every single day. It's great advice for anyone wanting to make progress in their career.

Cliff still didn't have the money to pay for full-time staff, however. 'I posted on a Facebook hackathon group called Hackers Europe saying I wanted to find reporters to write about Speechify and that I had this media hack I wanted to run. This guy, Simeon Kostadinov, messaged me from Bulgaria. And then a few weeks later, I posted again on Facebook saying I didn't have time to build a website, was there anybody good at HTML, CSS and JavaScript who could help me out. And this same guy from Bulgaria messaged me. I sent him a sketch, went to sleep, woke up in the morning and it was done. Then he starts helping me with the Chrome extension and he's like, how else can I help? I thought maybe he could help me hire people. So we got on a Skype call and I made a Google Sheet numbered 1 to 100, and when I woke up in the morning, he'd filled it out, made me a new Gmail address and had messaged all of the prospects. Eventually, I got him a visa, got him an apartment, moved him out to San Francisco from Bulgaria. At first, he worked with us as an iOS intern, then he became an iOS engineer, then head of iOS, and then he became head of engineering, and now he's COO.'

Cliff was able to pull in talent like Simeon at low cost because he was able to clearly communicate his vision for Speechify and enthuse people about it. He now has a core team, which includes his brother Tyler, who are all in their late twenties. And because they are young and free from family and property commitments, the Speechify HQ is a mobile one. Every six months or so, the company rents a town house in New York City, or a villa by the ocean, and the core team moves around the world. In total, the business has 120 people working in twenty-two countries. 'We don't operate on a nine to five basis. You just do the things that you committed to do. Everything runs asynchronously and everybody takes ownership and is very much self-directed.'

It's a system that is delivering results: Speechify now has 25 million consumers and they are gaining corporate customers with products that translate videos and podcasts or create voiceovers from a clone of your voice.

Cliff's team have built Speechify into a product that works on every device and every browser. Wherever there is text, Speechify can turn it into audio and Cliff claims they now have the second largest library of audiobooks after Audible, so it's possible you are listening to this using Speechify right now. And their customers aren't just dyslexics, of course. People with ADHD, second-language learners, blind users and time-poor users make up their core audiences. As the audiobook side of the business grows, increasingly their customers don't belong to any particular niche. Users pay a monthly subscription, which provides a healthy enough profit margin for the business to refine their product and invest to reach new customers.

'Facebook has almost two billion users, YouTube isn't far behind and TikTok will soon be at that level. If you get really good at advertising on those platforms, it's unbelievable. We have ten people working on data science where it's all about attribution, tracking, retargeting, etc. And we have a team that does creative, so we spend a ton of time learning from really good creators.'

With better ads, better targeting and better conversion, Speechify clearly has plenty of scope to grow.

While his team work on the product, Cliff is very sensibly working on himself, and I don't mean his fitness and health goals (though he has those).

'I used to say that I was a really good leader for fifteen people in a room. Then I wanted to become a really good leader for 100 people working remotely. For the most part, I've gotten very good at that, so now I need to work on being an excellent leader for like 10,000 people.'

I have no doubt that he'll figure it out. I love that Cliff has created a big business that initially set out to solve his own problems with dyslexia, but has grown to improve the lives of so many more people than he initially imagined. 'I'm on this earth to solve dyslexia,' he says. 'The goal of the company is to make sure that reading is never a barrier to learning for anyone, no matter what their background is.'

INSIGHTS FROM DR HELEN TAYLOR

Reading with your ears

The preference that Cliff shows for 'reading with your ears', as my colleague Susanna Cederquist calls it, and communicating orally, is common in people with dyslexia. I generally find that my own dyslexic students struggle to write down the same ideas that they can articulate brilliantly (though in a group setting this requires a lot of confidence, which doesn't always come easily to people with dyslexia, who have often been bullied and tend to struggle with self-esteem).

There are probably multiple reasons for this that relate to differences between written and verbal communication. Spoken language is more complex and more dynamic and is accompanied by action, body language and facial expressions. Studies also show differences in the neurological processes underlying speech versus written language. It is notable that once Cliff had teaching and learning approaches in place that suited his way of learning, he became one of the best-performing children in the class.

Strategising

As we will see repeatedly in these interviews, Cliff – like many people with dyslexia – is exceptional at strategising and coming up with creative ways to reach his goals. Strategising is all about navigating unknown territory and learning through exploration. This is reflected in the many creative ways he managed to overcome learning barriers, ranging from study groups and oral presentations to inventing his own text-to-speech software, the way he approached hackathons or the incredible way he went about building Speechify.

TIPS FROM JAMIE

1. Do the hard things first

Cliff knew that if he was to become the entrepreneur he wanted to be, he would have to learn to code. He dropped the subject he found easy – economics – and forced himself to take advanced coding courses. It laid the foundations for the success of Speechify.

The next time you write a to-do list, rather than putting them in order of preference, put them in a random order and label them in terms of difficulty, one being difficult and ten being easy. Now, action them, hardest first.

2. Don't take no for an answer

Dr Helen Taylor has explained to me that resilience in people with dyslexia might stem from our explorative nature. Explorers can spend a lot of time exploring and finding nothing: resilience is what keeps you exploring until you do.

For Cliff, this meant trying countless ways to learn to read before he struck gold with audiobooks. He did not wait for someone to send him a link to the answer; he went and found the solution. It can be hard to keep going in the face of knock-backs, but if you can keep your goal – learning to read in this instance – in sight, the rejections are kept in perspective.

And if that doesn't work for you, try reframing the narrative as Cliff articulated when he said: 'School is not happening to me; I am happening to the school.' Most people are passive, even with essential things such as health. If I need to change or do something for my health or my family, I'll find a way. I'll track down a specialist, I'll ask tough questions and, if necessary, I will be demanding too. Take ownership of what's happening to you, reframe the narrative and approach the issue again.

3. Think laterally

Approaching problems from new angles is something Cliff has mastered repeatedly. Think about his college applications or hacking a text-to-speech solution for reading. Lateral thinking doesn't always need to come from you: you can use your network. Write up a problem you want to solve and crowdsource the solution by asking others, directly or via a poll, to look at it from any angle they choose and suggest a solution. You will be amazed how quickly your problem gets resolved.

CHAPTER 2

KELLY HOPPEN CBE – THE DYSLEXIC DESIGNER

BUSINESS: FOUNDER OF KELLY HOPPEN DESIGN
QUALIFICATIONS: NONE

Kelly Hoppen is one of the most influential interior designers working today. Her clients include racing drivers, cruise-line operators, hotel chains and celebrities like David and Victoria Beckham. Her style – neutral colours and restful spaces – has been so successful that her surname has become an adjective: 'That's very Hoppen.'

Born into an affluent family in Chelsea, west London, Kelly grew up in a household where both her parents owned businesses. She admits it was a very lucky start to life, but when she went to school, she faced the same challenges that every dyslexic kid does. 'My entire life at school was horrendous because I thought I was stupid. I lived with this anxiety of not being able to read out loud in class.'

A diagnosis wouldn't come until adulthood, but away from academic subjects Kelly showed real talent, particularly in swimming and music, even though she couldn't read it. 'I used to fake it, and I used to watch others play and then memorise it. I found methods, I suppose.'

Her memory, it turns out, is phenomenal in other areas too. 'My mother pointed out to me recently that whenever she says do you remember so-and-so from my childhood, I always say, "What were they wearing?" It was only recently that I realised that was me beginning to find a way of coping with something. I still don't remember names, but I remember people because it's a mental picture, and I will remember what someone was wearing from twenty years ago.'

As we'll see, Kelly's visual memory has always been remarkable and it would prove to be a vital asset in the career she would go on to forge. Sadly, at the time, she didn't realise this might be a positive upside related to having dyslexia.

'I hated school, hated thinking I was stupid, but at the same time knew I had this ability to visually design. As a kid, my mum would ask me what I wanted to do on weekends, and I always wanted to go and look at show apartments that were for sale. I could then create worlds of my own. Everything was about the imagination. I lived in an imaginary world. I used to drive my mother crazy by constantly rearranging the furniture.'

At the age of sixteen, her life changed overnight when her father was killed. The shock would have blown most of us off course, but Kelly says it gave her purpose.

'I never ever, ever imagined my father would be killed. It was the biggest surprise of my life. And it left me with the feeling of, "I will never, ever not be in control of my life again." I wanted to make money, I wanted to be in control of that, to have security and I think that pushed me quicker into the world of work.'

An inheritance from her father was enough to buy a flat and allowed her to start a business, following in her mother's footsteps.

'My mother was my role model. She had a phenomenal business, and I learned so much from her. My grandfather was also an extraordinary businessman, so I'd always been surrounded by that. I've thought about this often, about children who are brought up in businesses where their parents work, and there's a work ethos. I think it's ingrained in you, so you can't sit back and do nothing.'

Kelly was born in South Africa – her family moved to London when she was two – and following her father's death, she went to stay with family for a while. She became friends with a group of musicians, and this led to an encounter with the law.

Her friends were black, and in apartheid South Africa they weren't allowed to stay in the same hotels as white people. They all tried to book into a hotel, but Kelly was so naïve she didn't realise that they legally couldn't stay in the same venue and snuck them into her room. She was arrested and spent a night in the cells. When talking to dyslexics, a recurring theme is a problem with authority, so I wondered if Kelly had a long string of rebellious episodes.

'No. I am so by the book. If a parking warden tells me I can't park there, I move somewhere else. I'm too scared. That doesn't mean I like being told what to do. If someone *tells* you to do something, it's very different from *asking* you to do something. I worked on Saturdays in the belt department at Harrods when I was growing up. It lasted all of thirty seconds, because I didn't like being told what to do. The same thing happened when I worked in Tilemart – I think that lasted ten days – because I was told to do something I didn't want to do, hence why I started a business.'

Kelly left school in the mid-1970s – aged sixteen – and launched her interior design business. She says she was lucky, as a girlfriend of hers was having an affair with a Formula 1 racing driver, who gave her a huge piece of work. But luck doesn't always, or even often, lead to success: that was all down to Kelly herself.

'I was tenacious, I was courageous and I believed that I could do it. For some reason I was good at networking. I wasn't nervous about talking to people, and I would ask people I knew for a recommendation for a builder, and I found my own network. There was no Google, you just had to talk to people, and I kind of faked it. I was a hustler and I think that's what being an entrepreneur is. Being a hustler means you're always looking for different avenues. And maybe because I was knocked-back badly at school, and my dad was killed, I suppose I thought what more could happen that was bad?'

Kelly built up an impressive list of clients and grew her business through word of mouth for almost two decades. Projects ranged from Kensington mansions to five-star resorts in Mozambique, to a beach house in Marbella, to a Gulfstream private jet and a VIP box at Twickenham Rugby Football Club. For many years she worked alone from home. When she became a mother, to daughter Natasha, and later a stepmother to Savannah and Sienna Miller – now a famous fashion designer and an actress respectively – when she married for a second time, Kelly finally hired an assistant to help, which made balancing childcare, working and doing the school run much easier. It wouldn't be until Natasha decided she wanted to join her stepsisters at boarding school that things really took off for Kelly's business.

One particular article in the *Financial Times* in 1996 led to lots of lucrative contracts. She was then invited to write a book by the legendary designer, and founder of the Habitat interiors stores, Terence Conran. *East Meets West*, published in 1997, focused on fusing elements of Asian design into European interiors and was a publishing success that brought a lot of attention. Kelly can pinpoint the moment when her name became a brand. 'Wedgwood approached me to start creating product and then a journalist wrote that, "this is very Hoppen". I was an adjective, so that was a defining moment.'

Spatial awareness is a trait often associated with dyslexia, but Kelly's is so finely honed that she can redesign a room – almost instantly – in her head.

'I can see an empty room and start to design it. It's like a grid effect and everything starts to appear in my mind. I can actually see the finished room, and then I can move things in my mind. I don't know where that ability comes from.'

I was interested to hear that Kelly believes all the senses are important to her designs. 'Smell is important to me, touch is important to me, sound. All of those things are so much a part of my world. I can walk into someone's home – it freaks people out – but I can scan a room within a second and know if something's out by a millimetre or if it should be moved or what would make it better.'

Sound, in the form of music, plays a pivotal role in her work as she can only design to music. 'When a certain type of music is on, it makes me feel good, which gets me in the mood to design. There are certain types of music and beats that resonate with certain people and looks. It's very hard, I just know that music puts me in a great space. I went into the design room this morning to look at something and the music was at a level where I couldn't even concentrate. When I go back there after this interview, my music is going on and I will be in that zone all afternoon. It doesn't work unless the right music's on.'

While designing a room, or a house, or a cabin on a cruise ship always came instinctively to Kelly, explaining her designs to clients was less intuitive, and so she needed to develop ways of transplanting her ideas into their imaginations.

'It was a real a-ha moment for me. I went to New York to work on an incredible project, and I'd designed the whole thing in my head. In my mind it was all finished, the nuts were in the bowls, the flowers were in the vase. And I got to the end of the presentation where I'd shown my client all the fabrics I was going to use and he turned to me and said, "I don't understand what you've said." How could he not see it? I told him again how it was going to be amazing, the sofa was going to be here ... but he just could not see it. That was the moment I realised that I had to paint a picture for other people. I started using visualists, artists who would draw the rooms for me. I'd sit down with them and point to where the sofa would go and tell them the colour, and if the pinks needed to be a bit redder. We went into every detail. Today, we've got CGI but it's still the same job, only then it would take ten days to create the visuals. Nevertheless, I learned that I needed to charge for it on every job. The artists would create these incredible watercolours – I still have all of them, they are amazing – and then I could say to clients, "This is going to be your living room."'

Designing a home for a client is inevitably an intimate process. As Kelly says, if you hire her, she's going to know where you keep your toothpaste and what's in your bedside drawers. That means getting on with clients is crucial.

'It's about building a relationship like any other. Everyone is shy and slightly reserved at the beginning, but I have this ability to ask the right questions to get the answers that I want. Then I start to build a picture of my client's life, and then I ask their partner certain questions to get a reaction from them. So, you've got to be a bit of a psychiatrist to work out what someone really wants. It's my job to make them feel completely safe and secure so that when they freak out, which they will, or get anxious and arsey and all the rest of it, I can guide them through it. The good thing is that I understand how vulnerable clients are when they open up their homes and their lives, so I get it. I feel it. I feel everything, actually. I'm a very sensitive person.'

Intuition and emotional sensitivity are closely aligned with dyslexia, so it isn't a surprise that Kelly tells me her intuition is 'off the charts'.

'I feel from the heart, I feel emotion in the pit in my stomach and I'm very instinctive. I can walk past someone in my office and know if something's not right. My team call me the white witch. I know when someone's pregnant, even if they haven't told anyone. Deepak Chopra says that feeling that you have is real. It's a chemical thing. If you walk past me in the street and I get a funny feeling in my stomach, it's not because you wanted to kill me, but you might have thought something bad about me as you've walked past and I felt that. When I read his book, *Synchrodestiny*, I knew I would never ignore those feelings ever again because I have them for a reason.'

Many dyslexics rely on their intuition, but Kelly takes it to another level. I wanted to know how this ability affects how she manages and builds teams. She currently has around fifty employees, some of whom have worked with her for over twenty-four years.

'I don't want people to come to work and feel like I did when I went to school; I want this to be a happy place. It's not just about employing somebody because they're good at doing something. If they don't fit in with everyone here, it's not going to work. All my team are friends and that's important, and once a month we do a pizza lunch together. It's an important part of my job to know the people around me, and if something doesn't feel right, you have to deal with it.'

The level of care Kelly has for her team can sometimes take a toll on her, as everyone feeds off her energy. She describes preparing to go into the office like preparing to go on stage. To make sure she's always ready for her curtain call, Kelly uses music to set her mood on the way into work.

'If a good Marvin Gaye song comes on, I'll walk into the office and I am, like, yes, ready to go. It's my job to bring energy and positivity, but that can be tiring and it can occasionally be lonely. You think everyone's your friend and everybody loves you, but you're the boss. The weird thing is I don't see myself as the boss, just as one of the gang, but that's me playing make-believe.'

As someone who says she had difficulties with maths at school, I wondered how her dyslexia impacts on dealing with the financial side of business. She accepts it's where she struggles the most.

'My finance guy does all these incredible spreadsheets, and I look at them and go: Woah. But he comes and sits with me and explains things, sometimes very carefully, in a way that I understand. It's like a different language to me. When you explain something like figures and numbers, I struggle because there's not an image to go with it, and my brain works visually. As he's talking to me, I forget the bit before because I can't see it.'

I wondered if that might make her vulnerable to staff or clients trying to get one over on her. She shakes her head. 'If push came to shove, I could figure it out, it would just take me longer. I'm very switched on about finance, and every Friday I get the reports in and I know every penny that's in every bank account, what it's for, what's going out and what money is coming in. I also have an amazing partner who's brilliant at things like that. I was very lucky to have been born into money, and I think there's a difference between coming from money and making money, and I have both. Plus, I work my butt off, so I know what should be in the bank.'

She told me a great story that illustrates how she's always had a firm grasp on the bottom line. She recently gave a talk to young entrepreneurs at Lloyds Bank and a guy came up to her beforehand and asked if she remembered him.

'I did. He'd been my bank manager when I was first starting out. I went, oh my God, yes, I used to bullsh*t the hell out of you to get overdrafts. That broke the ice with the young kids when I told them that story, but it's part of being an entrepreneur, that ability to hustle.'

But to hustle a bank manager successfully, you've got to have a sound grasp of the fundamentals, even if the details are a little foggy. Finance and spreadsheets aren't the only areas Kelly is relaxed about her team taking the lead on. She's happy to delegate most things if it gives her more time in the design room.

'If I needed to, I could do most things to run the business. I've just had three months without a PA and although I'm dying inside, nothing has fallen apart. Spellcheck helps – it would take my team a week to decipher my emails without it. I'm quite good at navigating situations and dealing with problems. With family, it's emotional, that's different, but when it's business, you can figure most things out. Sometimes when we lose a contract, the team will get down, but I'm always saying "but we've got this, and this, let's move onto the next thing".'

While I was with her, Kelly took a call from a prospective client and it was obvious when I went back into the room that it had gone well. She's clearly just as excited about her work work now as always. Knowing full well what her answer would be, I asked if she had any plans to retire. 'I'll never do it. Some things might change, but I'll never stop designing because that's what I love. I have a need for newness, for challenges, for the next thing. It's what keeps me alive.'

In 2013, a very big new challenge came Kelly's way when her agent got in touch and said that *Dragons' Den* was looking for new dragons and would like her to audition.

'I laughed down the phone because I just didn't think I would be worthy of doing that. It was such a big show. Anyway, I went and did it, and they called my agent up, said I was brilliant, which was so lovely to hear, and they signed me up.'

The closer it got to her filming date, the more the nerves got to her. 'Literally the week before, I was like, I'm pulling out. I can't do this. It was Duncan Bannatyne [who is profiled in Chapter 7] who actually calmed me down and said, "It's fine, because it will all be edited. It's not live. And if you invest in something and the due diligence doesn't work out, you don't have to go through with it." Someone else said to me, "You just come up with good one-liners, that's what will get into the edit." I was still very nervous, though.'

Even though *Dragons' Den* is edited, the dragons still have to assess a business opportunity with only the information the people pitching give them, and they have to make their decision on whether or not to invest in the studio. There's no going back to the office or leisurely reading the proposal at a later date. For someone who struggles with maths, I wondered if that was a challenge for Kelly.

'There was one time I had to work out what the percentage was, and I thought, oh my God, I'm so good, I've done it all in my head, and then Deborah Meaden butted in and went, "So, you're saying that your business is worth ..." I was out by about £2.5 million! Thank God I didn't say anything! I learned very early on that Deborah and Peter Jones would do all the numbers and figures for you, so I just had to look at the business and think, what could I do with it? And the beauty of *Dragons' Den* was that I came from a different point of view. I remember Deborah once saying that she'd made her mind up not to invest in a business, but then I'd come in totally left field, and now she wanted it. So, it's different minds, different skill sets.'

I can't think of a better example of why it's important for every business to have a dyslexic mind on their team.

'I miss it sometimes and still watch it avidly. *Shark Tank* too. I hadn't factored in that it wasn't just the twenty-one days of filming, which could easily be put into my diary. It was running those businesses. My thing was to invest in young entrepreneurs, because that's my passion, and they needed a lot more hand-holding. So I had to employ people, and it became a lot, so I had to step back.'

Kelly still does plenty of TV work, and she told me that sometimes stepping into a TV studio can make her feel like she's going back to school.

'If they say, here is the script, I start to sweat, I start to literally go back to being fourteen at school and failing. I'd go into panic mode when *This Morning* handed me a script, but I learned that I needed to say to the production team that I had to have twenty minutes in a quiet room where I could sit calmly and read it. I've taught myself that if I put an image next to each line and create a story, I'm able to actually remember it. Pictures speak volumes.'

It sounds almost identical to how I remember my speeches when I talk at events. Kelly's visual memory also comes into play when she needs to plan her day. Instead of making a list like most people, she draws mind maps and creates a visual representation of the tasks she needs to tackle. Intriguingly, Kelly's ability to visualise extends beyond three-dimensional design.

'I always visualised what I wanted my days or my year or my relationship or my friendships to be, and I visualised them to make them happen. This is going to sound very odd, but when I first read *The Secret*, I thought, well, hang on a minute, I wrote that.'

The Secret is a phenomenally successful self-help book that claims visualising success is the secret to bringing it about. 'I'd picked up that book and read it on a flight, I got off the plane and I literally was bouncing off the walls. I was like, woah, yes, this is real, someone else has written it.'

Despite her success, dyslexia can still occasionally pull the rug out from under her. 'I was once at a dyslexia awards lunch sharing a table with Richard Branson and Charles Dunstone from Carphone Warehouse. I thought, well, all these people have succeeded, and they've all got this. I've also been at some pretty big events with politicians and heads of industry, sitting in Downing Street and knowing I've got something important to say, but I get this imposter syndrome where I go back to my past, and I feel stupid and anxious and I have to really pluck up the courage to say something.'

I know how she feels: dyslexia, and those childhood feelings of being inadequate, can rob you of your confidence at any moment.

Kelly's dyslexia wasn't diagnosed until her daughter Natasha was tested at school. Natasha now works as a chef and cookery writer, another profession where dyslexic thinking often comes to the fore, and Kelly wonders if her grandson, Rudy, will also have inherited it.

'Natasha thinks he has, and so I started panicking, as his grandmother, because it took me right back to all the anxiety I had at school. What I really want, in talking about dyslexia, is to remove that anxiety for the next generation. But then my mind flipped back to watching him at six years old playing with a Rubik's Cube, and I went, no, he's going to be OK because that part of your brain is so powerful when you're dyslexic.'

INSIGHTS FROM DR HELEN TAYLOR

Autobiographical memory vs facts

Kelly exemplifies how dyslexic people seem to have better recall for autobiographical 'stories' from their pasts with contextual information (episodic memory) than for information stripped of context, such as individual names or numbers (semantic memory). This may be due to trade-offs in how the brain processes information. We need more research to verify, but rather than a way of coping with difficulty, as Kelly thought, this may be an innate strength. Indeed, richer episodic memory is associated with richer 'episodic' simulation: the ability to imagine and mentally search through possibilities, something at which Kelly is clearly exceptional.

Complex mental models and simulation

Kelly's design process is particularly interesting in how she 'sees' an empty room and starts to design it. Dyslexia research is lacking, but we can infer possible insights from other research on search and learning

Exploring to develop knowledge about the unknown is much more effective with prediction. To predict, we need internal mental representations or models of the world. These are built up through our everyday experiences.

It is likely that Kelly has built up such mental models of different designs throughout her career, and before that by visiting show homes, learning what works and what doesn't. One idea being developed is that mental models of *familiar* environments are part of a larger overall map that encodes information to support exploration in *novel* environments.

In other words, Kelly's experiences and models may collectively inform how she populated an 'empty room' in her imagination. Using these mental models we can search through possibilities using the episodic simulation mentioned above. Reflecting this, Kelly describes how she mentally plays with room configurations to create different 'imaginary worlds'.

TIPS FROM JAMIE

1. Practise visual thinking

The next time you're in a meeting, try giving your episodic memory a head start by making a note of what people are wearing and how they look (you can have some harmless fun with this: e.g. 'looks like my first boyfriend; the jumper they were wearing looked like my gran's sofa'), as well as the important things they say. When you return to your notes, the visual anchors will make you recall more details of what was said.

2. Find other inputs

You can help your brain develop different solutions by giving it different inputs. Try resolving your next problem by standing up or using images, touch, sound or movement to understand the problem. If you're still stuck in a rut, collaborate with others for a diverse viewpoint. Many heads are better than one.

3. Use music to set a state of mind

Musical anchors are a great way to put your thinking into a particular state immediately. We all have tunes that, in just a few notes, can flash you back to your first school disco or favourite holiday.

Create playlists that you can play when you need to engage different types of thinking. I have my writing playlist (no lyrics), gym playlist (drum and bass) and a work from home playlist (folk, rock, R&B, pop and hip-hop). They instantly help me achieve the right state of mind and put me into a state of flow.

CHAPTER 3

WILFRED EMMANUEL-JONES MBE – THE DYSLEXIC FARMER

BUSINESS: FOUNDER OF THE BLACK FARMER
QUALIFICATIONS: NONE

For Wilfred Emmanuel-Jones, dyslexia was the least of his problems growing up. In the 1950s, aged four, he emigrated from Jamaica to Birmingham, England. His father swapped his job as a community pastor for work on automotive assembly lines. Angry both at his loss of status and the racism he faced, his dad took it out on his family. And with eleven of them in a two-bedroom house, there was no escape from the violence.

'I always felt like an outsider. I never felt as though I belonged. When you factor me being dyslexic, being black, coming to a different environment, you can understand why a lot of people I went to school with ended up in prison. I'm sixty-six now, and I look back and see those are the things I needed in order to become entrepreneurial. They were very, very painful at the time but they also really toughened me up.'

School was particularly hard. 'It was an environment where I couldn't read or write and it was a pretty traumatic experience. In those days, they used to be able to cane you and every week I would be in the headmaster's office, so much so that even he got fed up with it. The worst punishment I ever had was I had to stand outside his office for two weeks. So I'd arrive in the morning, and I would stand outside his office until four o'clock every day for two weeks.'

Another teacher punched him in the stomach, while a third told him that during the war 'he had shot better men than you'. It's truly shocking. Wilfred never once got the impression that his teachers cared about either his welfare or his education. 'It was one of those classic inner-city areas where they were really just policing rather than educating you. I was very disruptive in the classroom and I made the teachers' lives a misery.'

One of them locked him in a stationery cupboard for the duration of a lesson. 'I spent that hour tidying up the cupboard and he was so shocked when he let me out. That was actually a key moment, because that teacher could have seen that I had something about me that wasn't just aggression and violence. My response to anxiety and stress is still to tidy things up. There is something about me that wants to create order out of a chaotic situation. In one sense, you could argue that that is the essence of entrepreneurialism.'

Like so many other contributors to this book, Wilfred didn't hear the word dyslexia as a kid. What he did hear was that he was thick and stupid.

'I spent a lot of time hiding it and feeling really, really ashamed. Kids want to find some form of weakness in you and I was very mindful that if they found any weakness, they would just annihilate me. So I had to spend a lot of my time hiding it. I would do anything to try and get out of reading out loud. If I had been timid, people might have been sympathetic, but because I was an arrogant little f*cker, I just pissed people off.'

His best memory of school was being in the school play. 'I played Moses, and everybody thought I did a really good performance. Maybe that was a tiny nugget of someone thinking this guy's got something about him, but I spent most of my time being a truant.'

You won't be surprised to learn that Wilfred left school without any qualifications, but that doesn't mean he wasn't without ambition. The most tranquil place in his life had been his father's allotment and it was there that he first had the idea that he wanted to own a farm. His second ambition was that he didn't want to replicate his parents' lives.

'When I was very young, about eleven years old, I made a promise to myself. I said there's no way I want to be like these people. And by "these people" I meant my parents. I'm a believer in mindset and I just knew that I would do everything I possibly could to not be like them. From a very early age, I realised that I was an outsider and I was on my own. And that developed a mindset that if you're going to do anything in this world, it's going to be down to you.'

Without a role model, or anyone to take him under their wing, Wilfred chose what felt like his only option to get out of Birmingham: he joined the army.

'They did terrible things to me at school, but they did even worse things to me in the army. You can imagine in those days, being a black guy who's mouthy and difficult, you're going to get your head kicked in. They did some atrocious stuff to me, and eventually I got kicked out. I didn't want to go home, so I was on the streets for a while until my sister let me stay with her. The first eighteen years of my life was a pretty brutal existence.'

Absolutely broke, Wilfred didn't even have the bus fare to get to job interviews, so he walked. By the time he got there, he often found that the position had been taken. He eventually landed jobs in kitchens, either washing-up or flipping burgers.

'The important thing about my story is that everything has been absolutely audacious. I remember saying to everybody in those kitchens that I wanted to get a job in television. There was a documentary series called *40 Minutes* that I loved and I thought I would enjoy making television programmes. Everybody around me thought I was nuts because it was very much an Oxbridge-type profession. Who the f*ck did I think I was? But, thinking outside the box, I went to the Pebble Mill studios in Birmingham and asked the security guards if I could open the gates for them. From that, I met the cleaners and from them I met a producer called Jock Gallagher, and he saw something in me.'

I wanted to know if Wilfred thought his audacity was linked to his dyslexia. 'What I've had to do is bluff it all the way. As a kid I realised I had a choice to either shut up or bluff. A lot of dyslexics I've met choose the quiet option so as not to be made a fool of, but something in my personality wouldn't allow me to shrink. I always had bluster, was always trying to force my way in.'

From these initial connections, Wilfred forged a career for himself and went on to spend fifteen years at the BBC, mostly making cookery programmes, working his way up from runner to director. 'I was very talented, and the reason people like Jock took me under their wing was because I would go the extra mile. They knew I would do whatever it took to come up with a film.'

It was also Wilfred's job to break in new talent, including giving a first TV break to one of the most successful chefs on the planet: Gordon Ramsay in his appearance on the British documentary series; *Boiling Point*.

'Back in the day we used to shoot on film, and film was very, very expensive. You needed a director who was pretty strong. But then video came in, which is very, very cheap and you didn't need directors in the same way. You could just send somebody out with a camera and it'd be all put together in the cutting room. I realised there wasn't going to be much future for somebody like me in television, because I didn't have the skills to be a producer.'

And the reason he didn't have those skills was his dyslexia. 'You had to be really good at writing scripts or treatments. It just was impossible, so the dyslexia meant I had to leave the BBC.'

Around this time, Wilfred embarked on two new adventures. First, he met and married his wife, Michaela, just three months after meeting her. And secondly, together, they set up a food marketing agency.

'Rational people often use words like ''impulsive'' and mean it as a negative. What I would say is that I make very, very quick decisions. I'm very, very impatient and I'm a great believer that the more time you spend thinking about something, the more likely it is that you're not going to do it. I work on the basis that you will not know all the answers at the start, there will be lots of problems that will come your way and you'll figure it out as you're going along.'

It's not clear, but I'm pretty sure he's talking about both marriage *and* business.

Wilfred's background in kitchens and food programming meant starting an agency for food producers made sense. Apart from the small detail that he didn't have any clients.

'But I did have a lot of balls, and I put in a lot of hard work to get my first clients. I think I drove people mad and got them to the point where they thought they'd give me a break. I didn't really see myself as an entrepreneur. I regarded myself as being a creative. I've always needed a sense of creating something. And what I mean by creating something is doing something that challenges convention, and marketing is about being courageous and being bold. If you want to get people's attention, you know you ain't going to do it without taking a risk.'

The solution was to work with challenger brands, and back in the mid-1990s those included Loyd Grossman sauces, Kettle Chips and Cobra beer. However, once they got established, the extra management layers they inevitably acquired meant his once upstart clients were less likely to embrace his creativity and they moved on to bigger, more corporate agencies. Wilfred wanted more control over his own destiny, and his childhood dream to own a farm came to the fore when he was on holiday in the West Country.

'I wanted to buy a farm and I happened to be around Devon and Cornwall when it was pissing with rain, so I started looking at properties. I had no idea about whether it was a good location, but I just thought, I'm going to go for it. The farm was a manifestation of the desire to have some control over my life. As someone brought up in such chaos, the big driving factor in my life is: how can I be in control rather than battered around? One of the things I like about being on my farm is that it's tangible. This is my piece of England. When you look at the aristocrats and they have all these vast lands, there's some power that goes with that. It makes me feel like I'm not a nobody, that I'm not on society's scrapheap.'

Even though Wilfred bought the farm at a good price, he now had the immense challenge of making it pay for itself and had to turn his land into a profit.

'I remember standing in the garden and saying to myself, you've done it now boy. The interesting thing is at the moment you've achieved something, there's always a bit of an emptiness, that feeling of, well, what now? And that's when the idea for the Black Farmer brand came about.'

As someone who'd been marginalised by society, Wilfred knew he wanted to create and own something mainstream.

'Everything I've done all my life has been a big battle not to be stereotyped. If you're a black kid, if you're dyslexic, if you're from Birmingham, the instinct is to stereotype, so I always wanted to be mainstream. I didn't want to create a brand that people thought was just for black people, that they thought was an ethnic minority thing. So I thought what could I do that was mainstream and I came up with sausages. What could be more mainstream, more *British*, than a sausage?'

Wilfred had the pigs, and the pork, but he didn't have the skills or infrastructure to make the sausages himself, so he started speaking to manufacturers. Once the product had been perfected, his next task was to come up with a brand name.

'I was thinking for ages about what to call it. Back then all of my next-door neighbours used to call me the Black Farmer. I just thought, actually, that is a bloody good brand name because it has an edge to it. You know, in this age we live in where people are really nervous about using the correct language – can you refer to people as black? There was a real nervousness about it, but that's the edge you need. If you want to get people's attention, you have to stand for something. I actually don't really see myself as a businessman. I see myself as somebody who's bringing about a change; it just so happens that business is what allows me to do it. I wouldn't be excited to just run a business for its own sake; I want to know how my business is going to make a change.'

Food and farming are two of the least diverse industries in the UK, so he was creating change without doing anything else, but Wilfred wasn't interested in creating novelty: he wanted to create a legacy.

His sausages were created for the upmarket supermarket Waitrose in mind. It didn't matter how many phone calls Wilfred made, or meetings he talked his way into, he couldn't get Waitrose or any of the major supermarkets to stock his sausages.

'People didn't get it. "Are these sausages just for black people?" Time and again they said they weren't interested, but what I realised is that the only people the buyers feared were their consumers. So I decided to do a massive sampling programme at these big country fairs. I put all the buyers' names, telephone numbers and email addresses on my website and told customers that if they liked my sausages – and they did – to ask the supermarkets why they weren't listing my products. I was lucky, it was just when Facebook was taking off and that new technology gave me an edge.'

The first supermarket to list Black Farmer produce was mid-market Asda but Waitrose kept saying no. 'The only reason they eventually gave me a listing was because I said to them, "Right, if you don't list these sausages, I'm going to take an ad out that says Waitrose refuses to list the Black Farmer." So they listed me. They resented it, but they listed me.'

Wilfred's brush with respectability didn't stop at upmarket retailers. In 2010, he again overturned convention by standing for parliament as a candidate for the right-of-centre Conservative Party, where I can imagine he ruffled plenty of feathers. Wilfred didn't win the seat of Chippenham, but politics' loss was farming's gain. His business diversified into other pork products and then eggs, then mail order and now a new chain of urban farm shops, with a flagship store in the middle of Brixton market, which I have visited and love.

He also runs his own start-up incubator that he calls his 'hatchery'. Often working with his employees who've had good ideas, he'll set up a joint venture and help them build their own businesses. He says the strength of the Black Farmer brand opens a lot more doors than these guys could open on their own. One of his ventures is the Gym Kitchen range of ready meals, another is a Swedish meatball business he values at £10 million. He's also working on a halal venture.

'It's my philosophy, and it's been my experience, that we have to help each other to grow and develop. If you're on a journey of change, I will help you. It's one of the things I absolutely love doing. I'm not really interested in just giving someone a job. The moment you employ somebody who's only interested in a job, they want to know about terms and conditions and the hours. I'm not really interested in people like that. I don't really look at qualifications. I don't even look at experience, I just try and understand a person's mindset. A degree means jack sh*t to me: I want to know what's in your head and how we will work together.'

Two of Wilfred's children are dyslexic, and their school experience couldn't be further from his own. 'I knew that when I had children I would never send them to a state school. I didn't want them to go through what I went through, so I sent them to really posh private schools. That said, I didn't want them to go to an academic school. I wanted them to go into an environment where they could come out with confidence, and I realised that is what the private school system gives you. And if you have confidence, you can achieve anything. It's not qualifications that matter, it's confidence.'

As someone with no previous experience of private schools, Wilfred made sure his money was well spent. 'I remember the school saying that my daughter – who had already been diagnosed with dyslexia – wasn't performing. I went bloody ballistic. I am paying you a sh*tload of money and it's your goddamn job to educate her. I told them I wanted a weekly report on her progress, which they duly sent.'

These days, Wilfred's daughter is a qualified clinical psychologist, so she obviously got the support she needed. 'That's the thing about dyslexia, with the right support, it can make a fundamental difference.'

Wilfred's commitment to changing the conversation about dyslexia has led to him becoming an ambassador for the British Dyslexia Association. 'It's a passion project of mine and I do a lot of talks at schools.'

One of the things he's most excited about is the ability of technology – from spellcheck to text-to-speech to dictation – to change the experience of being dyslexic. 'I compensated by being hard-nosed. I always needed someone to write a letter for me, or write an email; it was a bit of a handicap. Technology now means all of those things don't really matter at all.'

While this is great for the next generation, Wilfred still wonders what a difference it would have made to him. 'I look at my life and, actually, I could have been a more phenomenal success if I hadn't carried this fear, this guilt, of being dyslexic. If I didn't have that, I could have been really, really successful.'

He's selling himself short – he's been successful by any measure you care to use – but he makes a really important point. If we can, as a society, remove the fear and guilt that so many dyslexics still feel, we will unleash a vast well of untapped potential. And if technology simultaneously allows dyslexics to achieve their potential, then we have lots of reasons to be extremely positive about the future.

INSIGHTS FROM DR HELEN TAYLOR

Dealing with uncertainty

Wilfred was very comfortable figuring things out as he went along. People with dyslexia often revel in situations where there is a lot of complexity and uncertainty as they have faith in their ability to learn through exploration and figure out new solutions. Indeed, it is in highly complex environments with many variables that exploratory learning adds most value.

Many of the interviewees have been able to visualise or imagine what the long-term outcome is they are wanting to achieve. We see this very clearly in how Wilfred marketed his sausages; he clearly knew what he wanted and he was highly creative in coming up with different ways to get there. We also see it in how Cliff figured out ways to read and learn. Coming up with a long-term vision can also inspire creativity as it provides a clear objective.

Inspiring change

It's notable that Wilfred describes himself as 'somebody who's willing to bring about change', which is apt as the purpose of exploratory learning is to enable change and adaptation. It's not the business he's interested in as such, but rather the change that business can make. His exploratory nature is also reflected in the diverse ideas he came up with to expand his business. But he didn't stop there. He started 'hatching' new businesses with his employees. As we'll see several times in this book, dyslexics are often serial entrepreneurs, instigating change and then moving on to the next venture.

TIPS FROM JAMIE

1. If at first you fail, pick yourself up and try again

Wilfred's life story demonstrates the immense value of resilience. He also shows us that resilience often comes at a personal cost. Negativity from others could have easily pushed him off track. If you feel this happening to you, try this simple trick. The next time you find yourself surrounded by negativity (or, better still, before you enter a negative environment), imagine a colossal glass bell jar dropping over your head, covering your whole body and sealing with the ground. Then, picture other people's negativity bouncing off and leaving you in a positive state of mind.

2. Connect up

Dyslexic thinkers love the challenge of getting from A to Z and, if possible, missing out on the B to Y. One of the best ways to do this is to connect with people who are more experienced and often better than you. My question is, who have you been putting off connecting with for fear that the more experienced, wealthy or famous sit further up some mythical ladder? I challenge you to communicate with them today, do something for them, ask for help and see how this might accelerate your growth.

3. Make others shine

As a TV producer, Wilfred quickly realised that his job was to make others shine. By doing this with Gordon Ramsay, he realised that this skill would serve him well in other walks of life. In a world – especially on social media – where we are encouraged to promote ourselves, what can you do to make others shine, and how might that be reciprocated to benefit your growth? Try it: give your local shop a Google review, your friend a LinkedIn endorsement or your partner a thank-you note that can be pinned to the fridge.

CHAPTER 4

EDWARD KEELAN – THE DYSLEXIC VENTURE CAPITALIST

BUSINESS: INVESTOR AT OCTOPUS VENTURES
QUALIFICATIONS: MBA

I start the interview with Ed by asking how old he is. 'Forty-three,' he says, then immediately corrects himself. He's forty-two. 'That's a classic dyslexic thing where you don't even understand how old you are. People think, surely you should know that, but my memory doesn't work like that. Things like that just don't stick in my head. I don't know why, they just don't.'

I laughed because I often get my age wrong too. If Ed has a reason to know something, he'll absorb the information easily, but if he can't see the point of knowing something, the data often doesn't stick. He had the same problem at school.

Of all the interviewees in this book, Ed has probably attained the highest level of education – an MBA from Oxford University, no less – but the struggles he had at school meant his mum had to fight for him to even sit his GCSEs.

'Can you imagine, as a ten-year-old, getting your work back from your teacher and it's just got red pen all over it? In every paragraph – I still have some of my school books – over half the words are spelled incorrectly, and at the bottom the teacher has written, "You must use a dictionary, Edward." Some of those words didn't even have the right first letter, so how much use was a dictionary going to be? How long would it have taken me to look up thirty words?'

Ed was sent into the lowest set in the school and took his classes in huts on the grounds, away from his mates. To this day, he still feels the shame of being 'sent to the huts'.

Something was clearly wrong, but he didn't know what that was. Neither did his mum, but she knew that Ed wasn't thick and she went to the school to get him moved into a higher stream.

'The school thought that being in the lower set would help me as I'd get more time, but the trouble with being in the lowest set is you can only do the lower papers when it comes to GCSEs, which means you can't then get your A levels, which means you can't then go on to university. I find this idea that you break children into clever and stupid at a young age, without understanding them, immoral.'

The anger Ed feels at kids being put on the scrapheap at such a young age is apparent on his face, and that's part of the reason he is now a governor at his old school.

The family moved from the Midlands to Hampshire when Ed was nine. His father – Irish and independently minded, and almost certainly dyslexic – had a clothing manufacturing business that needed to pivot when globalisation meant most fashion brands moved their factories overseas. 'My childhood was surrounded by Levi jeans, but when Levi moved their operation to Malaysia, my dad started making riding gear, jodhpurs and the like, with a specialist company in Winchester.'

Within months of moving there, Ed's dad realised the new factory was too large for the operation and suggested they rent out half the building. The riding company realised he was right, but they also worked out they could be more profitable if they moved their entire operation to Asia. His dad could have gone with them, but he didn't want to move the family.

It was a tough period for the Keelans, who had bought a house at the height of the market and faced double-digit interest rates on their mortgage. His dad started selling insurance door to door, and his mum got work as a dinner lady.

'I remember Mum and Dad saying that when the recession of the 1990s was over, things would be better. We had this terrible rickety old caravan that Mum and Dad used to just park up in a random field, and we'd have these amazing holidays. I remember thinking, what could possibly be better than this?'

His dad's insurance business expanded into other financial services and he eventually qualified as a financial adviser. Aged fourteen, Ed helped his dad with his accounts.

'I was brought up around entrepreneurship and I couldn't understand why anybody wouldn't want to be an entrepreneur. I think entrepreneurship's the best thing: you take something that does not exist, and you create something. All of a sudden, these people are employed, and all of these lives are affected.'

Ed went on to study for a degree in business at the University of Hertfordshire, thinking that he would also start his own venture. His course included a year's placement, and rather than working in the UK, he wrote to hundreds of companies in the US asking for a job. The British-American Chamber of Commerce, based in San Francisco, said yes and paid him a salary of £10,000.

'I spent my year meeting people from the British Consulate and British companies that were trying to set up in California. I was playing golf with CEOs of Visa, and I was talking with senior directors of Bank of America and British Airways. I had zero idea that access to that type of person for a nineteen-year-old was just insane.'

Ed showed some entrepreneurial flair while he was there. He suggested that they seek sponsorship for their annual directory. His boss was dubious about the proposition but offered him 50 per cent of the profits if Ed could get a sponsor. Ed did and pocketed a $5,000 bonus. He also suggested that they sold memberships to the organisation at their Christmas dinner. Again, his boss was sceptical, but Ed earned himself another bonus. Ed might have been an employee, but he was demonstrating entrepreneurial instincts by challenging the status quo. His willingness to suggest a different way of doing things – classic dyslexic thinking – would be a hallmark of his career. Nevertheless, creativity is a label he's wary of using.

'The stereotype of the dyslexic is, oh, you must be really creative. My sister, who is not dyslexic, is a phenomenal artist. My wife, who is a chef, is an absolute artist; again not dyslexic. Me, who is dyslexic, has got no sense of style. My wife will ask me about decorating a room and my answer is whatever you want because I can't really tell the difference.'

Ed's dyslexia might not test the boundaries of design, like Kelly Hoppen's, but he is constantly pushing at the limits in other ways, identifying opportunities to make systems better.

Back in the UK, Ed's plan was to start his own business when he graduated – he had an idea of opening a chain of barber shops – but during the 'milk round' where blue chip companies recruit the brightest graduates into their trainee schemes, Ed was offered a job with Rolls-Royce. Even on his first day, Ed could see how he wanted to do things differently.

'Somebody random from HR came to address the new recruits and I was like, this doesn't feel right; that's not how I would do business. To me, that culturally just wasn't right. Surely the chief executive should be doing it?'

When the underwhelming HR representative asked who among the new recruits was thinking that Rolls-Royce would be a career for life, Ed was the only person who didn't put his hand up. He did his financial planning qualifications in his spare time with the intention of joining his dad's business, but only once he had proved himself at Rolls-Royce.

He left the company within a year to join a start-up and was the first employee at KorteQ, a tech operation that helped organisations manage their corporate knowledge. This gave him a front-row seat to what it takes to get a business off the ground without the financial risk of being an entrepreneur. 'You've got to be brave, and that's the other thing I love about entrepreneurs is that they're willing to take that risk.' Technically, Ed is still an employee, but he has demonstrated entrepreneurial traits in every job he's ever had. 'I don't know if I haven't had the right opportunity to start my own business, or just that the time wasn't right.'

KorteQ's founder grew the business to a million-pound turnover with ten employees, but in Ed's opinion, his unwillingness to delegate meant the business remained stuck at that level. It was around this time that Ed met up with a friend from San Francisco who mentioned he was considering a move from accountancy into venture capital.

'I didn't know what it was. He explained that you take a pot of other people's money and decide what small companies to back. I thought working with lots of new businesses sounded amazing, and then he told me that VCs sit on the board of these companies and help manage them. I was like, "And that's a job? You literally get to invest capital in entrepreneurs, work with entrepreneurs all day, and then help them grow?" Immediately, that's what I wanted to do.'

A university friend worked in the IT department of Octopus Investments, a relatively small investment house with eighty employees, and he suggested Ed join his company. He applied, and after *ten* interviews was offered a job in the sales department selling Octopus's funds to financial advisers like his dad. It wasn't the job he was after, but he hoped to make connections and eventually manoeuvre his way into the company's investment department.

Ed says that until you've done telesales, you don't understand resilience. It's hours and hours, if not days, on the phone cold-calling people who mostly don't want to speak to you.

'I talked to the best sales guy and asked him for advice. He said, it's really easy: "Even if you're twice as good as me, I'm still going to beat you because I make ten times as many calls as you." That really resonated for me. I've always thought people will outsmart me, but no one will outwork me. There's a real fashion for working smarter, not harder, but trust me, the ability to work until two in the morning and get a job done counts for more than somebody thinking a bit smarter than you.'

Ed told his colleagues that he wanted to be an investor, but everyone said he didn't stand a chance because he was a salesperson on the operational side of the business. Traditionally, that was a barrier people didn't jump over.

'That side was for privately educated kids who have gone to Oxford and then gone on to a Big Four accounting firm. It's not for some kid that went to a very average university and worked their way into a sales role.'

To get the job he wanted, he knew he had to impress. At the time, Octopus was a relatively small outfit. Today it incorporates Octopus Energy, the UK's second largest electricity supplier, but back then it was possible to have a direct link to the CEO, Simon Rogerson.

'I think that's where dyslexic thinking helped. I didn't just do the sales job, I also went to Simon and told him the way the sales team was organised didn't make sense. I came up with a structure that divided the country up by postcodes and gave each field representative a section of the country. I think that's quite a dyslexic thing, where you're not comfortable with the status quo being the best way of doing things. I want to say, "Let's do it differently." I knew the only way I was going to step into the next role was to work really hard and come up with new things.'

When a coveted promotion didn't materialise, Ed decided to resign to find his way into an investing role, but Simon asked him to stay and launch the sales side of a new investment product. Within months, Ed – who was a fully qualified financial adviser *and* the son of a financial adviser – knew the product wasn't going to fly. So he resigned again, and again Simon asked him not to and offered him another role. Octopus was at the beginning of its move into energy, and Ed's new job was finding ways for the business to invest in solar energy.

'They said, right, we've got all this money to invest in solar, but we've got no solar plants to invest in. We figure you'd be the best person to go and find those solar plants. Can you go and call farmers?'

Unsure exactly what he could achieve, Ed set up in a new office, got a phone line installed and called a few farmers and asked if he could pay them to put solar panels in their fields.

'A few of them told me to go away, but some were interested in leasing an acre and eventually I built a sales team of about twenty people. I then I organised all the grid connections and the planning permissions, and so became like a solar developer. It's the hardest I've ever worked; it was nine months of the absolute hardest graft ever. I was getting in the office at 6 and was not back until 11.'

It still wasn't the investment job he wanted, although it did feel like his own little business within Octopus. Simon told him that he intended to launch an energy supply business – Ed thought it was a terrible idea; clearly, he was wrong about that – and Ed realised he was becoming an energy investor, which wasn't part of his plan.

'Although I was a part of the leadership team in the energy division, it had never been part of my design so I quit again. I'd decided it was the time to take over my dad's company. I even wrote a business plan.'

Simon had other ideas, however, and put in a good word for him with the head of a new department within the investment division. Ed's new boss knew of his reputation as a hard worker and gave him a six-month probation as an admin clerk on the new team. It was a demotion, and a significant drop in salary, but Ed nevertheless said yes. He had just welcomed his second child into the world, and many people in his situation would have turned the opportunity down. 'It wasn't quite the ventures team, but it looked a little bit like the ventures team and I was happy to take the pay cut and demotion because I was on the right ladder.'

Many wouldn't have even seen it as an opportunity. They'd have been insulted that they were expected to do the filing and take the minutes. Of course, as a dyslexic, Ed found taking the minutes hard.

'I asked if I could record the meetings, but because of their confidential nature, people were too paranoid about what might be said. Those minutes could get used in court if things go wrong, so it would be problematic to have that sensitive information recorded, but I just found a way. I think that's the thing with dyslexia, you just find a way of doing things. For starters, I got very good at typing and would write notes furiously. I was doing it three times a week, and at the beginning it was awful, terrible. I'd write everything down, scribble everything down in my notepad as fast as I could. Then I started writing the minutes without looking at my notes. Because of the way my brain puts things together, finding themes and patterns, I could very easily go, well these were the key points and this is what really mattered, and that's what went into the minutes. I would then look through my notes and see if I'd missed anything. A lot of the time I'd leave things out because they were not important. I now tell new recruits to write the minutes without looking at their notes, but no one ever listens.'

Ed slowly climbed the ladder on the investment team, rising from administrator to analyst, then associate, manager and finally principal partner. He had always worked with smart people, but Ed noticed that the brains on the investment side of the business were even sharper. On the sales side of the business, his ideas to shake up the systems had been well received, but on the investment team he found that there was less scope to innovate because everyone else was already having brilliant ideas.

'On the investment side, everyone is so smart. I could outwork people in other parts of the business to get ahead, but I couldn't outwork people in the investments team. Everybody in the investments side works really, really hard and is also super-smart, genius-type people. I felt massive imposter syndrome about the fact that I'd been to a not particularly good university or not got an accounting qualification.'

Ed's solution was to study for an MBA, which he looks back on as a crazy decision now as his second child had just been born. Nevertheless, Ed arranged with Octopus to spread out the sabbatical he was entitled to over the course of a year, and by using up all his holiday allowance, he was able to study and still work full time.

'My wife was very supportive, even though I was working in my shed until two in the morning. I wanted to do it because I'm just a massive business geek, and the idea that you could go and learn about business from Oxford University and be part of that ecosystem … why would you not do that? I know a lot of people think MBAs are nonsense, and they don't help you, but if you're a business geek and you get to learn from the best professors about marketing, and about finance from the best people in finance, why would you not want to go and embrace that and be with an incredible peer group?'

He gave it every minute he had and estimates he put more hours into a part-time, two-year MBA while having two young children than he did for his full-time undergraduate degree. When Ed posted on LinkedIn that, as a dyslexic, he'd earned an MBA from Oxford University – something that every teacher he ever had would have thought was beyond him – the response was extraordinary. He had hundreds of messages from contacts all over the world both congratulating him and thanking him for being honest about his dyslexia, saying it gave them hope for themselves and their kids. He also posted photos of some of his schoolwork, complete with the unhelpful comment from his teacher to use a dictionary.

Ed finally got the job he wanted in the ventures team after more than a decade at Octopus and is now a partner specialising in investments in B2B software businesses. He says his skill is in seeing the big picture more quickly than some of his colleagues. Given the high percentage of his colleagues who went to Oxbridge, it's a fair assumption that only a few of them would have faced the academic challenges that dyslexia poses. The investment world is not a very diverse place, and he stands out – even as a white male – on the basis that he went to a state school. Ed uses this status as something of an outlier to his advantage.

'If I'm in a management meeting, I'll ask an entrepreneur about how their business works, whereas my colleagues will probably be more into the data. I'm able to A) grasp the concept of what the problem is that the company's trying to solve maybe a bit quicker; and B) then also try to see the opportunities for that company and what it might be able to do.'

He gave me an example of one of his favourite investments, a business few people will have heard of called Countrywide Healthcare Supplies.

'Talk about unsexy. They sell incontinence pads, rubber gloves, soap and things like that to care homes. My colleagues thought it sounded boring and their margins weren't great. But I was like, oh my God, this is amazing. They had customer relationships going back ten years in a market that's about to burst because of the ageing population. I thought that just their network of 20,000, 30,000 care homes alone had got to be worth something. Then we looked a bit closer and saw that the directors had stripped out all the dividends and none of the money had been ploughed back into the company. The branding was shocking. My view was that if we could rebrand, reposition it and put all the money that the directors were taking out back into the company, then there was something there.'

Ed thought they could sell direct online, maybe even start a subscription service for incontinence pads. Like he says, deeply unsexy, but it turned out to be one of their most successful recent investments, all thanks to his dyslexic thinking. 'Ninety per cent of all entrepreneurs think that venture capital offers them nothing other than money, but 90 per cent of venture capitalists believe that we offer more than just money.' Now imagine how much more money venture capitalists could make, and value they could add, if they hired more dyslexics.

That doesn't mean his team makes the right call all the time and being dyslexic doesn't make you an investing genius. 'They call the things you didn't invest in, or the things you rejected, the anti-portfolio. We looked at Huel when I was doing more B2C stuff and I was like, who wants dust through the post? Who is going to eat dust? No one wants to live off dust. And now Huel is a billion-pound company.'

Ed enjoys being part of the ventures team, but it took a while for his colleagues to recognise his strengths. 'Usually, when I start working with people they think I'm a bit odd, but after about six months they realise I'm quite good at problem-solving or I've got a cute angle on looking at a situation. After a while they go, he's quite useful actually. My boss now admits that in the first year he just did not get me at all. We've now worked together for five or six years, worked as a unit, alongside some other good people, and I think most people do now appreciate what I bring. It takes time because I'm not the traditional package, but successful teams need different characters.'

One of the things dyslexics are good at is recognising other people's strengths, and Ed is generous in his assessment of his colleagues. 'My boss is unbelievably shrewd and he's also really taught me about patience. I'll be like, get in there, get it done, but he says let's just take our time; let's know when to push, when to pull. He's the brakes. We're all really different, and I think that makes a good team.'

A good team still needs to find good companies to invest in, and Ed tips the scales in his favour by working as hard as anyone can to find the best opportunities. His logic is that if you only have a very small number of things to invest in, you'll find a reason to make those investments.

'What you need to do is build a massive pile of things to invest in because then you'll choose the best companies. You need to be out there burning shoe leather and finding those investments. It's not rocket science. When a good investment presents itself, it's pretty obvious that it is a good opportunity. The hard bit is making the networks and finding those opportunities.'

Again, his dyslexia works to his advantage. He says that a lot of investors are very analytical and feel uncomfortable about meeting people. They don't want to go out there and go to events, or cold-call people to see if they need investment. He takes a different approach.

'We get 5,000 to 10,000 applications for investment every year. But the percentage of investments that comes through from submissions is about less than half a per cent, whereas the percentage that comes from going out and finding them, through building a network, is about 5 per cent. That's a significantly greater chance of getting an investment through a warm investment than a cold one, and therefore you need to build that flow of warm investments and you don't do that by just sitting there.'

Despite his success, Ed's dyslexia can make him feel like he's right back in those huts in the school grounds. He avoids writing whenever he can, and gets anxious about meetings where he might be expected to use a whiteboard.

'I go straight back to the huts. There's this whole tussle going on in the dyslexic community right now between dyslexia being a disability and dyslexia as a superpower that can solve all of the world's problems. The truth is, we can problem-solve well, we can see big pictures well, which makes it really good for certain things, but what we can't do very well is look at the detail and write emails as well as other people. That moment, in front of the whiteboard, feels like hell. Dyslexia may give you other things that other people don't have, but it will also give you disadvantages that other people don't have to deal with on a daily basis.'

It's been a long time since Ed had an interview for a job, but he thinks you've got to be very brave to own up to your dyslexia on a job application. 'Whenever I mentioned dyslexia in interviews, I never got the job – I'm looking at you Standard Life and Accenture – but once I was in the door, I was fine and could communicate and explain my way through things.'

Ed hopes, as I do, that books like this will help change that narrative. 'Once you're in the meeting, you can share your vision. But if you struggle to put together the emails to get the meeting in the first place, then you need to find the right people to partner with. To this day, I still get my boss to read over important emails before I send them. If you're looking for investment, find somebody that can write your emails, and the pitch deck. The truth is that I don't know how many neurodiverse partners there are in the UK venture capital ecosystem. There are barely any state-educated people, let alone people who would have been cognisant of neurodiversity.'

Sadly, it's still the sort of environment where a spelling mistake gets you laughed at, and your proposal goes straight in the bin. 'It's really easy to say with dyslexia, don't worry about sending things with spelling mistakes, and don't worry about not having the finances quite in the right order. The truth is, you've got to understand what you're good at and what you're not good at. And the stuff that you're not good at, you need to have people to help you with.'

It's great advice, and I wondered when he might take the plunge and start a business of his own .

'The truth is, I love Octopus, and I've been really fortunate to work for a great company, under great leaders with a great culture. And I work with entrepreneurs all day, so I get my fix in that sense. Financially, it pays well, and it gives us a life that I could never have dreamed of. To risk that, giving away a job you love, working with loads of entrepreneurs you love, financial security for your family, because I've got an entrepreneurial twitch? It feels a bit of a selfish decision. But I do still think that I will at some point. Maybe when I'm fifty.'

That's if can remember how old he is, of course.

INSIGHTS FROM DR HELEN TAYLOR

Exploration in time

Global exploration also occurs in time. On the one hand, the further into the future you explore, the further you're exploring into the unknown. On the other hand, the closer to the present you are, the more you're dealing with things you already know about. People with dyslexia tend to struggle more with short-term time estimation and organisation. By contrast, they tend to be exceptional at exploring in time, where there is more uncertainty and complexity, searching through different possibilities in their minds to figure out the most likely future scenarios. Consequently, they can imagine the destination of their present trajectory, or how to change the direction of travel to reach a different destination.

We see both with Ed. First, it was immediately obvious to him that the market for care home supplies was about to 'explode' because of the ageing population: a connection that allowed him to see a business opportunity. In the case of his career, he could hold onto a long-term future possibility of being an investor. That long-term vision likely gave him determination in the present to enact the changes necessary for eventually achieving that goal, even if it meant sometimes taking a step back.

Identifying fundamental patterns and key points

This more global perspective is also reflected in Ed's minute-taking. Global and local perspectives are traded off – more ability in one area tends to mean less ability in the other. While local search and learning provide an in-depth understanding of a small area, a more global view means you lack the capacity to find or hold onto all the details. However, this enables you to detect more fundamental patterns and themes, as demonstrated by Ed's ability to identify key points and highlight what really mattered.

TIPS FROM JAMIE

1. Solve problems

It was President Obama who said his top advice for people looking for work was to 'be useful and learn how to get things done'. I could not agree more. Ed has shown his ability to do this throughout his entire career, whether by cold-calling farmers to acquire land or setting up complex sales teams. Society has far too many consultants, and we need more doers.

Finding a solution to a complex problem is a vital stepping stone to creating opportunity. Most of us have a good antenna for spotting problems, but only some are willing to use hard graft to solve them. If you're looking for a promotion or to expand work with an existing client, I'm willing to bet that if you ask your client or boss, 'What are your three biggest problems, and can I help solve one of them for you?', you'll be front of mind when the next opportunity arises.

2. Harness your emotions

Dyslexic thinkers are empathetic, both towards themselves and others. Ed is no different. His ability to control his ego, take a demotion and get a pay cut to enable him to follow his dream career is something most people would struggle to do. When you need to make a big decision, try making it with the view that 'I can't change anyone other than me'. This will immediately reframe your perspective from what you deserve to what you can influence.

3. Play the numbers game

I loved Ed's strategy of contacting hundreds of companies to secure a placement in the US. Most people would write to one organisation at a time and then wait for a response before moving on to the next. Ed's method meant he could have had several offers at once. It also means momentum is preserved. Where can you open multiple opportunities by making several approaches at once?

4. Look to add value

Ed shows that anyone can be entrepreneurial and add value to a business by being an intrapreneur – an entrepreneur who is a member of someone else's team. Where can you use your entrepreneurial thinking to add value to your organisation, family or community?

CHAPTER 5

THEO PAPHITIS – THE DYSLEXIC RETAILER

BUSINESS: FOUNDER OF THE THEO PAPHITIS RETAIL GROUP
QUALIFICATIONS: NONE

As a retailer and investor, Theo Paphitis is one of the best-known business leaders in Britain thanks to his time on *Dragons' Den*. He left school at sixteen after failing his exams and got a job as an office clerk in an insurance underwriter. His job was to write the risks on slips of paper and get them to the right assessor. At school, his inability to write well hadn't really mattered. Now a spelling mistake could be extremely costly.

'In those days, there were no computers. There were typewriters, but you had to write the 'line slips', the crucial bits of paper that went to the underwriters at Lloyds of London, by hand. I couldn't hide the spelling. I couldn't hide not being able to see the letters clearly. I knew the bloody alphabet, but in the moment, I just wasn't seeing everything.'

At school, he'd been able to fudge and bluster, but that wasn't going to cut it in the strait-laced world of insurance. 'My whole life, I'd assumed I wasn't bright because I couldn't read as fast as everybody else. I'd always had an inability to absorb written instructions and I assumed that was a problem with just me.' This feeling was reinforced because he had the same problems in Greek – Theo was born in Cyprus – as he did in English.

'That's what convinced me that it must be a problem with me. It's the same reading music, and because I thought these were issues with me, I knew it was down to me to find solutions to get around them so that people didn't think I was thick.'

The workaround on this occasion was buying himself a calligraphy pen as that forced him to take greater care with his spelling. When he confided in one of the secretaries at the firm that he was having trouble, she bought him a pocket dictionary, coincidentally from a nearby branch of Ryman's. He still has it to this day as it has huge sentimental value, because that secretary, Debbie, soon became his wife.

For people who struggle at school, the world of work can sometimes seem like a playground. When I meet dyslexic kids who are struggling, I let them know that if their brains aren't built for academia, they might be built for business. It was certainly the case for Theo.

'I was actually taken aback by how quickly I went from being terrified of not being able to get a job because I didn't know how to fill in a form, to feeling I had something to offer. Sadly, that insurance job wasn't the right one for me, but the rest of it? I loved it. I was engaging with people far senior to me, having discussions about things that were way above my pay grade, and in turn they saw this really enthusiastic, energetic problem-solving, gets-it-quick guy. Sadly, it was the same guy who was making an absolute f*ck up in some other areas, which were all in his pay grade.'

After a couple of years in the underwriting business, Theo realised he was going nowhere and when he saw an advert for a job that doubled his salary to £5,000 a year, Debbie persuaded him to go for it. The job was selling luxury watches in a subsidiary of Watches of Switzerland on Bond Street in London.

'I was an ambitious individual, so becoming a shop assistant was not where I thought my future lay. But I knew I wasn't suited to an office environment either, so I had to take a step back, which felt like a step down. I felt incredibly sorry for myself that the only job I could get was as a shop assistant, but on day one I went home grinning from ear-to-ear. I had found something that I was really good at, even after one day. And surprisingly, I loved it. I was talking to people, selling and strategising how I was going to sell something that cost – to me – several months' wages. The psychology of it fascinated me.'

He sold a watch for £1,600 on his first day, on which he earned commission, but the money was only part of the reason he was happy. 'Dealing with people and understanding people seemed to be my superpower. There were things I couldn't execute on my own, but I realised that if I worked with people, then we could execute them together.'

I wasn't surprised to learn that Theo has gift for sales. I don't know if the ability to sell is a dyslexic trait or an entrepreneurial one, but I asked him why he thought he was good at it. 'It's a vision thing. It's seeing a problem, or something you need to achieve, and breaking it down to the point where you know you can achieve it. By going bit by bit, you get the end result.' Which is another way of explaining that sales is all about removing the barriers to someone saying yes to whatever you are offering. A successful sale is concluded at the end of a sequence of solved problems.

Theo's next step on the career ladder was selling insurance policies, and from there he started selling financial products. He set up his own business – a two-man band plus a secretary – and moved on from brokering mortgages to complex re-financing for distressed companies. He became an expert at these negotiations and some of the deals were incredibly convoluted. Dyslexics are known for having an aerial view of situations, but Theo is also very able to dig into the weeds and deal with the details.

'I always start with a helicopter view, but I'm very determined. These days I have people looking at contracts for me, but there was a time when I didn't. When I had to look at a contract and I would start sweating. I would lock myself in a room and I would read it line by line by line by line. It probably took ten times longer than it would take anybody else, but at the end of it I would say I did as good a job as anybody. When you haven't got an option, that's what you do.'

Theo gave me another illustration of how hands-on he was in the early days. 'In my very early twenties a new computer launched called the BBC. It was joint venture between the BBC and the Open University and it cost £399.'

As we spoke, I was struck by how often Theo remembered the precise figures for almost every transaction, whether it was buying a computer forty years ago, or the sale of a recent business.

'My visual retention of numbers is ridiculous, compared to my visual retention of words.' He tapped his notebook. 'I've got some notes here that I don't remember, and I *just* looked at them, but I know exactly how much I paid for that computer. It was a lot of money back then, but I bought one and I taught myself to program in Basic. When I wrote a computer program, Debbie would still have to read it and tell me that I'd transposed this or that. Even when I was looking hard, I couldn't see what I'd transposed. Then Casio brought out a little programmable calculator that also ran on Basic, so I bought one of those too. Another hundred and fifty bloody quid.'

The reason he was spending the money, and devoting so much time to programming, was so he could then input all the rates and products offered by the banks into his computer. When you consider how difficult form-filling is for a dyslexic, this had the advantage of not just making his work easier, but speeding it up.

After several years in his twenties arranging loans for troubled companies, instead of putting a financial package together for one of the distressed businesses, he was asked to step in and become the CEO. Needless to say, he rescued the company and quickly got a reputation for turning around the fortunes of underperforming businesses. His love of technology then led him to start a mobile-phone retailer in the early 1990s. That venture really took off when they started selling their phones inside branches of Ryman, the high-street stationer. When Ryman itself ran into cash-flow problems, Theo was the perfect person to take over the business.

Under his leadership, Ryman went from making an £8 million loss to an £800,000 profit inside a year. You can't turn a company around that quickly on your own, and his success is a testament to Theo's ability to persuade the team he inherited to do things differently. He did that by visiting the shops and warehouses and talking to his staff. When he took over the lingerie brand Contessa a few years later, he did the same thing. His ability to make a personal connection, to actually go out and talk to people, is a classic dyslexic behaviour.

When Theo heard complaints about staff having to pay for their own tea and coffee, he not only supplied the drinks, he put microwaves and fridges in the stores for staff to use.

Some business leaders I've witnessed over the years are quite good at hiring staff but not very good at leading them. They confuse their team with contradictory instructions, or they micro-manage them and forget to thank them. Not only is Theo adept at delegating to his teams at work, on the home front he leaves everything to Debbie (or Mrs P, as viewers of *Dragons' Den* will know her). From house-hunting to dinner parties to holidays, it's clear there is a very clear division of labour in their marriage.

They married when Theo was only eighteen and I can't help but wonder if it's significant that Debbie was the first person he really confided in about his spelling.

'Like me, she'd hardly had any formal education, but she could spell anything. A Scrabble player extraordinaire. Amazing handwriting and a memory like an elephant, so now I knew my problems weren't just down to the quality of schooling I'd had. She always says to me that I was the brains, but in the early part of our relationship, she was. She could execute what I wanted. We'd often have a little discussion, then she would do all the form-filling and the organising. Then, when we started living together, she sorted out the letting agreement, mortgage agreement, getting the electricity and gas. She did all of that because I struggled with it. But in the workplace, I found that because I'd gone through school having to problem-solve all my issues, I didn't have the same problems. As soon as I found a problem, my mind immediately wanted to find a solution. It might not even have been my problem, but I still want to find a solution to it.'

That same instinct can mean that Theo doesn't shy away from an argument. 'If I believe in something, that's it. I will argue for it till the end. I hate injustice. It drives me flipping mad. When I see an injustice, then I have to call it out. I can't stand by.'

While you'd expect a man worth £300 million to enjoy spending his money, Theo was a spender even when he was younger. He has always driven nice cars and bought houses right at the upper limit of what it was possible for him to borrow. But he also talks about having 'walking the street money', by which he means having enough ready cash to take advantage of an opportunity that might come his way.

'I have a very healthy amount of paranoia about going back to having nothing. So healthy in fact that it borders on the unhealthy. Whatever I do, I get obsessed by it. If I was to take up gardening, I would be obsessive about it.'

This means that when he starts something he always finishes it. It's not typically a characteristic associated with dyslexia, but it is fundamental to success.

'The struggles I had at school taught me a lot about persevering, about finishing, about delivering something and getting it done. I couldn't worry about how long it was taking somebody else to do something, I just had to deliver it in my own time. And I learned that if somebody else can do it, then I can too. And now I can never leave anything unfinished. I've been on a diet recently, and just to leave food on the plate hurts me so much because it's unfinished.'

I wonder if his need to complete tasks also stems from his competitiveness, a trait that helps explain why Theo thrived in one of the most competitive environments imaginable, *Dragons' Den*.

Although the programme we see on TV is heavily edited, in the studio the Dragons still only get half an hour or so, maybe an hour, to decide if they want to invest tens of thousands of pounds of their own money in a new venture. It's actually the perfect environment for a dyslexic thinker because you have to take a helicopter view, you have to assess the entrepreneur who's pitching, you have to analyse the figures *and* you have to make a quick decision, something that inevitably means trusting your gut instinct.

Before Theo entered the Den, he had bought and sold many businesses through lengthy weeks of negotiations and contractual box-ticking. I wondered if that background was helpful when he suddenly had to make decisions within the hour.

'I've bought multi-million-pound businesses where I have made the initial decision on the back of an envelope. In some cases, I've had to raise finance for those deals, and most banks are not happy to lend you money with a business plan on the back of an envelope. So I've paid somebody to take my envelope and put it into a fundable business plan. Believe you me, even after they've done all the analysis, and all the sensitivities, and everything else to justify their numbers, they pretty well always came out and agreed with my envelope.'

This balance between intuition and analysis is a key component of business success. 'I can sense things, I can feel things, I can smell things. I can ask the right questions. That's why, when I got on *Dragons' Den*, it was easy. There were huge egos, massive egos of successful people in that room, all fighting for screen time on every pitch, thinking of the right questions to ask.'

After nineteen series, the programme is more polished and has changed since Theo quit in 2012. 'It was quite raw in the early days, and it was very similar to real business. Sitting in that chair, with the other Dragons, and having to interrogate entrepreneurs and ask the right questions, work out the numbers and do a business plan in my head, but it was easy.'

I wondered if, despite his success, Theo felt his dyslexia still held him back. 'Do you know what? One of the great things about getting just a little bit of success is that you build up the confidence to say "get lost" instead of being hurt. Because do you know what, it's not important. It gives you the confidence to say it's an issue, sure, but it's not an issue I'm bothered about. They might be *my* spelling mistakes, but it's *your* problem.'

That's true whether or not you've achieved a certain amount of success and it's something every dyslexic should feel able to say when someone makes fun of their spelling. My own dyslexia has a quirk: while I'm not great at spelling and grammar, I'm weirdly really good at picking up mistakes in other people's writing. It turns out it's not a trait Theo shares.

'You could send me an email with forty errors in it and I wouldn't spot one of them. So long as I understand what the email is about, and so long as people understand me, I'm not going to worry.'

Theo hasn't had a formal diagnosis of dyslexia, but when his eldest son was tested around the age of eight or nine, a very large penny dropped.

'To be honest with you, it had never even occurred to me that I was dyslexic. I just knew I couldn't spell and that sometimes I saw words back to front so I had to read everything twice. I had just thought it was to do with the way I had been schooled, but when my son was diagnosed, it was a light-bulb moment. "You mean this is a thing? It's got a label?" I had no idea. Would I rather have not had those problems as a kid? The answer is yes. But if I wasn't dyslexic, I might have passed an exam or two. I might have gone to university. And then I might have done something really boring.'

While dyslexia can get you sent to the back of the class in school, in the world of work, it can also be a passport to a much more interesting life.

INSIGHTS FROM HELEN TAYLOR

Understanding previous behaviour in order to move forward

Dyslexics seem to have an aptitude for understanding complex systems and bringing about change. This is also apparent in how Theo went about persuading his teams to do things differently. In order to instigate change in complex systems such as social groups or businesses, we need to develop an understanding of what already exists and how it came to be. Theo sought to gather this information from the best possible source – his shops and warehouses – and personally gathering stories from people who made up the existing business. Undoubtedly, this understanding enabled him to change the trajectory of the business.

Reading people, groups and situations

Theo, like many people with dyslexia, feels that understanding people is a real strength. This may be due to particular talents in active listening and non-verbal communication. Studies indicate that people with dyslexia possess greater emotional reactivity. They also often possess an exceptional aptitude for being able to 'read' a room, notice subtle gestures, expressions, body language and other non-verbal cues. This, combined with an ability to connect the dots and understand the different people involved in a situation, as well as the broader context, can translate into talents for negotiating, persuading or intervening to avoid a dispute before it escalates.

Such skills are extremely powerful in helping people with different perspectives meet in the middle or changing minds, as demonstrated by Theo's ability to persuade his teams to work differently. We also see this when people 'go with their gut' when hiring. It's likely they're unconsciously picking up and interpreting non-verbal cues that contribute to their quick decision-making.

TIPS FROM JAMIE

1. Keep asking questions

People with dyslexia are known for their curiosity because they constantly explore, a theme throughout Theo's career. Unlike many other contributors in this book, however, Theo's exploration led him to locate distressed assets to buy, rather than businesses to start or problems to solve. It clearly demonstrates that you don't need to be an inventor or the first to be successful in business and life.

2. Build your confidence

The quote '*They might be my spelling mistakes, but it's your problem*' is brilliant, but it takes some confidence to do that. But here's the thing: confidence isn't something you have; it's something you *do*, and the more you practise, the better you become.

If you are dyslexic, the most powerful day of your life will be the day you tell people and advertise the fact you are dyslexic. So do it: update your LinkedIn profile with the skill 'Dyslexic Thinking' and add a line to your email signature like the one I use – '*I have the dyslexic edge: expect simple spelling errors and brilliant ideas.*'

3. Take a helicopter view

Are there any radio stations who still use 'the eye in the sky' helicopter to report on traffic? Or have we all moved to the global network of satellites beaming live travel information directly to our devices? The concept, however, is the same. When you're stuck in traffic, it's challenging to know what's causing the hold-ups, how long they'll last and if there's an alternative route. With information from a couple of thousand feet (or a couple of thousand miles above us), the problem looks much more straightforward.

What Theo does brilliantly is assess the whole landscape in a snapshot. Customer, product, price, distribution, staff, etc. Only after he sees the entire perspective does he get into the details. What does the helicopter view of what you're working on look like? Think in terms of your overall health, wealth, business or contribution.

CHAPTER 6

PAUL ORFALEA — THE DYSLEXIC PRINT BILLIONAIRE

BUSINESS: FOUNDER OF KINKO PRINT
QUALIFICATIONS: DEGREE

If you're a certain age and you lived in the US towards the end of the 20th century, I'm pretty sure you'll remember Kinko's, the vast chain of copy shops. If you're under twenty-five, there's a chance you won't even know what a copy shop is. Over three decades, Paul Orfalea, the son of Lebanese immigrants, built the business he started with a $5,000 loan into a billion dollar giant of US retail. No wonder he's now in demand as a professor of entrepreneurship at several prestigious colleges in his native California.

As the child not just of immigrants, but of entrepreneurs, Paul always knew he'd start his own business. His father and maternal grandmother were both in the clothing business and his first job was working in his father's factory.

His teachers had very low aspirations for him. One even told his mother not to worry too much about him because one day he thought Paul could learn to lay carpets! Other teachers might have been surprised by even that level of success: Paul went to eight schools and was expelled from four of them. He was considered so backward that when he was in the third grade (aged eight or nine), he was sent to a remedial class where the other students had Down's Syndrome. An IQ test result of 130 got him back into mainstream education. Paul isn't surprised his teachers despaired. His own mother referred to him as 'the problem child'.

Paul wasn't just bullied at school by other pupils, the teachers beat him too. 'Sister Sheila? I flunked her second grade and she paddled the f*ck out of me for two years with a ping-pong paddle. Then I had Sister Madonna and she hit me on the calves.' Paul got hit at home too. 'My mother hit me with a strap. My brother used to torture me, and he was good at torture.'

Despite all this, Paul says he enjoyed school, he just didn't see the point of learning and told me that because he didn't see any purpose for algebra, he couldn't comprehend it. It didn't help that his mind would wander.

'I never knew how to control myself. I really did not know. And then I was at this new school and I thought, if I can control myself right now, I could prevent myself from getting in trouble. And it was just like an epiphany.'

He graduated from high school with a major in 'wood shop', a solid D average and came eighth from bottom out of a year of 1,200 students. He has a diploma that looks the same as everybody else's, it just doesn't have the little extra stars on it like *cum laude*. It was enough to get him accepted into USC in Los Angeles.

'I wore my tie and went to see the admissions officer and I brown-nosed, right? I got accepted and then I figured out how to get through college. When the class catalogue came out, I went to the professor who taught the football players and said, "I'd like to be on your waiting list." And the professor said, "Well, I never thought about having a waiting list. Sure, you can be in my class." So, I got into all the football players' classes, where they lowered the curve. I could easily get a C in those classes.'

What he really studied at college, he says, were loopholes. He even managed to pass a literature class that, in his words, was run by a hippy. Apparently, all you had to do was show up and you got a C.

No employer ever asked to see his academic credentials because Paul had already started Kinko's by the time he graduated. He was photocopying papers for a friend in the college copy centre when he noticed how busy it was. His girlfriend at the time was studying at a college in Santa Barbara where he knew they didn't have a copy centre. He didn't bother writing a business plan or doing market research, he just went to Santa Barbara, found premises near the campus and called Xerox to lease a photocopier.

'It was the lunchroom of a restaurant, no bigger than a garage, which the owner charged me $100 a month for. Then I figured out I was the main artery of the campus, and every student needs notebooks and pens, right?

So, I put spiral notebooks and pens on the sidewalk. Back in those days, film came in a cartridge, and I did photo film processing also.'

Photocopying was a relatively new technology in an era before the personal computer and home printer. Only big firms had photocopiers, so any teacher or college professor who wanted to hand out sheets to students needed a copy shop. And if you wanted to send out your résumé to several employers, or submit a manuscript to publishers, unless you wanted to type it out several times, you needed a company like Kinko's.

Paul would have been able to fund the business himself had he not just lost his entire savings of $5,000 in a bond market crash. The fact that, as a teenager, Paul was investing in the stock market tells you that he was already taking finance seriously.

'The summer before I started, I lost every f*cking penny in the bond market. That really hurt. I swear to God, I'm still pained over that bond market crash. So, my dad co-signed a loan for me from a bank for $5,000.'

This was despite the fact that his father thought the business had as much chance of success as a fur company in Death Valley: he couldn't understand how you could make a profitable business charging 4 cents a copy. Paul quickly proved himself to his father. After taking out the loan in September, he had repaid it in full by December the same year.

The name for the business was Paul's nickname at school, which he'd been given because of the kinks in his hair. Paul believes that business names with strong consonants, like Google, Xerox and Kodak, are easier to remember. 'If I'd called it Orchid, you'd say, what flower was it? Carnation?'

Kinko's got its first customer before it had even opened its doors. A professor in a hurry saw his A-Board on the sidewalk, knocked on the door and placed a $50 order. Paul quickly realised that he wasn't in the copying business, he was in the *problem-solving* business. Putting his customers' needs first would be the route to his success.

Cash flow was greatly helped by the fact that Xerox didn't invoice him for the first year. 'They were so screwed up. They'd never bill you. I swear to you. It was such an easy business to start. All you did was plug in a Xerox machine, build a counter and ring a register. I had cash flow from day one. I bought $1 million worth of machines from Xerox and I kept waiting for the invoice. Lo and behold, it came a year after we started getting the machines. They were so screwed up in their billing, but that's what really built the business.'

Paul says he had a vision of still working in the shop after twenty-five years, serving the children of his current customers when they started college. He knew he didn't want that to be his future. He realised the way to make sure someone else was behind the counter was to start another branch and grow. Not everything was plain sailing, however. Paul noticed that his competitors were offering printing – not just copying – services, so he bought a printing press for his second location.

'It was just a nightmare. That was a hard thing to manage. We got a blueprint machine, a camera, a printing press, a darkroom. All things I didn't know how to run. Maybe in California we're a bit flakier because the guys wouldn't show up if the surf report was good. And when something went wrong, the printer guy would blame the camera guy, who'd say, no, it's the printing press that's broken. It was impossible to manage and I remember going to the accountant when I was really broke. He said, "Why are you doing this? You're never going to make it." That was a dark day. I was really in a hock with everybody. But the low-hanging fruit was the copier, so I just ate the copier business.'

At Kinko's third location, Paul ran into a different kind of problem. 'I went to the store about eleven o'clock in the morning and the manager wasn't there. I knew I had to figure out a smarter way of getting people to work better, so I started doing a profit share with incentives and recognition. I had no other choice but to get them self-motivated. If I put up $2,500 and they put up $2,500, I had them. When they brought in their own money, they were invested in that business. I didn't need their money to open up the locations, but I needed them to be invested.'

When Paul had worked in the first Kinko's store, he was very rarely behind the counter, choosing instead to be on the shop floor. By the time he had several stores, he was rarely at his desk in the head office either, as he had become the company's Head Wanderer. And when he was wandering, he didn't just visit his own stores, he looked in on his rivals too.

'For every one of mine, I went to five competitors, observing what people were doing right. You can't make money while you're in that office worrying about the things that are going wrong. You make money by seeing, oh, there's a good application there. Oh, I like the way they're filing the paper there.'

Paul never turned up at his stores unannounced. 'It would undermine the morale of the manager. You have to respect your managers. Besides, I knew who the f*cked-up people were. I didn't have to go unannounced. You can see it in their eyes. Honestly, I could walk into a store and the eyes of the workers told me if it was going to be a good or a bad visit. Do you want to know what the telltale sign was for a good store? The breakroom. That's where you saw how well the manager communicated with the workers. How neat it was and how they posted their goals in a clear and succinct manner.'

Paul had many achievements with Kinko's but the one he says he is most proud of is that it was frequently voted one of the best places to work by *Forbes* magazine. He created a great atmosphere, in part, by leaving his team alone. 'Do you know what the best definition of management is? It is to remove obstacles. My job is to make your job easier and mostly that means getting out of your way.'

This worked at the head office too: Paul was wandering so much he was rarely there, and that meant his team had to make decisions without him. This was decades before mobile phones, or even faxes. His team had no way of getting hold of him and had to wait for him to dial in from whichever motel he had checked into (he says he wasn't a fan of five-star luxury). The upshot was they learned to problem-solve without him.

The fact that store managers were also often part-owners of the business certainly helped with their motivation to work hard, but Paul thinks there's another reason why Kinko's was a good place to work.

'This was the real motivator, and I saw this in the very beginning: a customer walks in and they're always on a deadline. Maybe they're a senior person talking to a young person, and the senior person doesn't know how to do something and the young person suggests a solution to the senior person, who then gives them some validation for being good at their job. At the end of the process, they get a thank you from the customer. And they can see that their work has something to do with planet Earth. Like helping somebody get a job, or printing posters to help find a missing child. There was an abducted little girl in Spokane, Washington, and the family went to the police department first and came to us second. With that kind of stuff, our team really felt what they're doing contributed to society. All I had to do was get the f*ck away from that relationship.'

Kinko's initially opened in locations on or near college campuses, but as more and more people needed copying services, the business expanded to main-street locations using the same partnership model. Some partners ended up with more than a hundred stores, meaning that within Kinko's there were several large partner-owned businesses. Paul also had a wholly owned subsidiary from which he retained 100 per cent of the profits. In keeping with his hands-off approach, this company was managed by a president who ran it on his behalf. He kept a flat management structure, with all the subsidiary presidents reporting directly to him. He's keen to point out that this wasn't a franchise operation. As he says in his autobiography, *Copy This!*, a franchisee/franchiser relationship can often be confrontational. 'The franchisee has an expectation that the franchiser will make him successful. I wanted our co-workers to know their success depended on them and not on head office.'

Paul had some strict criteria when selecting potential business partners. Unsurprisingly, they had nothing to do with college diplomas or relevant work experience. One of them – an ability to save money – was taken care of by the need for them to put some cash on the table. Another way he whittled away partners who wouldn't suit Kinko's was punctuality. If people turned up late to a meeting, that was an immediate black mark against them. He took the time to get to know potential partners over drinks and found out if they had kids, or wanted them, if they got on with their parents (he figured if they didn't, they had a problem with authority and wouldn't get on with him) and talked about anything other than work. He also watched to see how they interacted with their server or waiter and would always throw in a random question about something like the Chinese

cultural revolution to see if they bullsh*tted a reply.
He had a policy of not hiring bullsh*tters.

Once people were hired, Paul's philosophy wasn't to
manage them, but rather to manage the environment
they worked in. Did they have the right perks and
benefits? Did Kinko's make it easy for people to make
their 401 (k) contributions (a US employer-sponsored
pension contribution scheme), for example. After his son
was born with a congenital heart defect and died at
just seven months, Paul realised how important it was for
parents to be near their children, so he built a day-care
facility next door to their office for his co-workers. They
offered scholarships so that co-workers could apply to
send their kids to college. If the environment was right,
with the correct guard rails and incentives, he found that
his teams didn't need micro-managing.

Kinko's kept innovating and although some of their ideas
didn't work out, like large-format fax machines, others – like
opening twenty-four hours a day – were transformative.
Understandably, store managers were initially resistant to
the open all hours strategy, but often teams were working
late processing orders anyway, and students pulling an all-
nighter or companies meeting a deadline were loyal and
grateful clients. Revenues jumped by between 10 and 50
per cent at the 24-hour locations.

The firm expanded internationally after a Japanese
MBA student, and Kinko's customer, at the University of
Michigan wrote a paper suggesting his employer and
Kinko's form a joint venture in Japan. The student sent

Paul a copy as a courtesy. Paul thought he was on to something and asked him to set up a meeting with his boss. Not many businesses would take a college essay seriously, but Kinko's first customers, and many of their employees, were college kids and Paul had learned to take on their feedback. In fact, when he started teaching at the University of California, one of the tests Paul would set his students was to go into a branch of Kinko's and suggest ways to improve his operation.

As the business grew, Paul found himself in more and more meetings. Let's just say it wasn't his natural habitat. Like a lot of dyslexics, he found them difficult. 'I'm really disruptive. I can't sit still. I met this guy in my forties who said he stopped going to meetings and became much more effective. I should've listened to him. Apparently, if you doodle or chew gum it helps, but I could never sit still.'

Paul's dyslexia was also problematic when it came to reading reports. 'I designed mine to be one page so I could see clearly what the hell was going on. New people came in and they had seventeen pages of bullsh*t. I had to insist that people be brief and concise.'

Paul didn't even keep those seventeen-page reports. He had filing cabinets in his office but they were all empty. By not getting bogged down in the details, Paul claims he was able to be 'on' his business rather than 'in' it. That's a terrific way of explaining the helicopter view associated with dyslexic thinking. He nevertheless found the responsibility of running a big business stressful.

'I was stressed all the time. When you get a big company, all the workers are so confident in their future, but as the owner you're sitting there going, I'm not quite sure about this. Every year of my life that business was for sale.'

When the laser printer was launched, Paul saw the writing on the wall. 'Let's say you wanted to put a little blue on your paper, I'd have to charge you $1 a copy. But I was at my sister's, and rather than going to a copy shop, she did 200 flyers for her real-estate business on the laser printer. And I thought, man, I better get out of Dodge.'

After thirty years, Paul negotiated to sell the business to a Wall Street private equity firm. Or as he calls them, 'The dumb sh*ts of New York.'

'I think there is an arrogance that comes with a certain education. They go to elitist high schools, then on to colleges: Princeton, Harvard, Yale. They view people like me as a bunch of dumb sh*ts. Well, I always viewed them as a bunch of elitist dumb sh*ts. They have a contemptuous attitude, but thankfully my brother is a banker and he knew how to talk to those kind of people. Bankers always thought I was a little odd. But my brother could talk their language, so he was our point person.'

Paul became a phenomenally wealthy man when the deal went through. He was on holiday with his first wife and two children when he got the call and for the next eight or nine months he says he had a fabulous time. But then he started to realise the new owners were making changes he didn't agree with, and, as chair of the board, this led to clashes.

'I realised they were incompetent pieces of sh*t. They fired really good people and brought in this organisational chart that was too complicated. The Catholic Church is a billion people and they have a priest, a middle manager called a bishop or a cardinal and the Pope. Basically, three layers. We had to have four! I'd go to the field and no one was accountable. I'd ask what the problem was and they'd go, oh, it's not me, it's that layer up there. When I ran that business, man, I could point fingers and they knew they were accountable. And people like to be held accountable.'

'I found myself in endless meetings. The New York guys would just go over the report they had sent me and take this little laser-like thing and just point at the numbers that were already in the reader. I was f*cking bored to pieces. All these prominent people were on the board and they were just zombified.'

Kinko's was sold again, in 2004, to FedEx for $2.4 billion, at which point Paul stepped back entirely from the management of the business, though he still retained some of his shares. He had already done some lecturing at California colleges, and this became a bigger part of his life. He is now a visiting professor at the California Lutheran University's School of Management, the University of California and the University of Southern California Marshall School of Business, among others. He has also taught classes at NYU, Princeton, Harvard, UCLA and the Wharton School of Business. Needless to say, Paul's classes aren't like anyone else's.

Instead of getting his students to write papers, he gets them to talk to each other. He's been known for setting assignments that require students to ask each other out on dates and he doesn't accept any essay that's longer than a single side of paper. I wanted to know if this was an approach his students appreciated, so I spoke to Joe Rapaport, a recent alumnus of Paul's Entrepreneurial Mindset course at USC who is dyslexic himself.

'Instead of having a lecture, we would sit around in a circle and, basically, we would ask questions. He gave out reading assignments, but he always made sure that they were short and comprehensible. Before each class, we would have to prepare questions and we'd go around the table just asking questions. He would be stern about how we were asking questions, and ultimately his lesson was: it doesn't matter whether the question is a good question or a bad one. You want to present yourself confidently. You want to reduce the "ums". And you want to be able to provoke emotion. It was very conversational. He didn't shy away from his differences and his troubles, and would talk about his dyslexia and his ADHD all the time. Working with him, and being challenged by him, really helped me feel more confident about being a dyslexic entrepreneur.'

Joe has set up Kenko – apparently the name is a coincidence – a platform for physical therapists and their patients that drastically reduces the recovery time after accidents. Joe had the idea for Kenko while recovering from a back injury, and he took Paul's course with the intention of turning it into a business. Not only did a fellow student become his business partner but, under Paul's guidance, Kenko has got off to a rocket-fuelled start. 'We did a pitch competition, won third place and got some money for it and used those funds for development.' They got second place in another pitch competition and that led to them working with the accelerator programme at Sunstone Investment.

Joe is twenty-nine, and his success demonstrates how transformational a good mentor can be. Paul shows the same level of care for his students that he did for his employees. Joe told me that Paul takes the time to stay in touch with him, either going out for lunch or even just a message or text.

'He puts in that time and effort, and it's not only for me, but for the thousands of his students. He's definitely been a great role model, who I hope to emulate in the sense of being an influence for future generations, especially with children who have dyslexia.'

Paul really enjoys his work in business schools. 'I honestly can't think of anything cooler than being a college professor. It's so much fun hanging around young people. You don't have to do much: I talk and they listen.'

Paul might not think he's doing much, but students like Joe clearly disagree. With his impact on businesses like Kenko, Paul's influence over the next generation of entrepreneurs could prove to be an even more remarkable legacy than his incredible success with Kinko.

INSIGHTS FROM DR HELEN TAYLOR

Understanding systems at a global level

Global exploratory learning ability in dyslexics often manifests as an ability to understand on a holistic scale. Often, this is an aptitude for understanding complex systems and how they change over time. This is worth explaining, since understanding such complex systems is where dyslexics excel.

Complex systems consist of many interdependent, networked parts. Interdependence makes their behaviour difficult to predict if you only look at one part at a time. Some systems are more than the sum of their parts and can only be understood holistically and contextually. Examples include ecosystems, social groups, and of course businesses and the economy.

In Paul's case he worked out the most efficient, effective organisational structure for optimal communication and accountability. We also see this in Edward's chapter when he recognised the most efficient global-level configuration and, accordingly, reorganised the sales team across the whole country.

Seeing the whole picture

This global view is also reflected in the way Paul researched the broader context of his business by visiting the stores of his rivals, or by avoiding getting bogged down in the details of reports and documents. As he put it, he was able to be 'on' his business rather than 'in' it.

Not micro-managing ensured he was instead able to maintain an overview of the business that he was able to develop over time.

The global, or holistic, approach he took to his staff is also fascinating. He considered his employees from many different perspectives, from appreciating that surprise visits would upset them, to motivating them through personal investment, appropriate perks and benefits, to supporting their children with day care and college scholarships. He effectively designed a whole employee experience that would facilitate motivation and loyalty.

TIPS FROM JAMIE

1. Use intuition

Paul makes the start of Kinko sound very simple. He had a need and his intuition told him others would have the same need, so he found a shop and gave it a go. Business really can be that simple, and I rarely hear people who trusted their gut complain about getting it wrong. If you have a gut feeling, trust it, give it a go, just protect the downside. I have made nearly all my decisions to start or invest in a business based on intuition, and the investments my gut told me to walk away from have all failed.

2. Keep it brief

The shorter the explanation or the report, the better the content. Paul's idea of having everything on one page rather than 'seventeen pages of bullsh*t' achieves two things: it makes the person writing the report think more clearly; it also helps the person reading the report to gather the vital information in less time.

The next time you're communicating a proposal, report or update, ask yourself what can be taken out, how you can make this brief and give yourself a goal of saying what you need to say on one side of A4 or in the first two minutes.

3. It's good to talk

One thing I've noticed about dyslexic thinkers is we talk more than we write, and it's clear from speaking to Joe Rapaport that Paul's students prefer this. The next time someone asks you for an update, drop them a note and ask, 'Can I do this in person?' But don't forget that you have two ears and one mouth for a reason!

CHAPTER 7

DUNCAN BANNATYNE OBE — THE DYSLEXIC HOTELIER

BUSINESS: FOUNDER OF BANNATYNE'S HEALTH CLUBS AND HOTELS
QUALIFICATIONS: NONE

Duncan Bannatyne is a well-known entrepreneur thanks to his time on *Dragons' Den*. The 75-year-old Scot is still the CEO of the health and hotel businesses that bear his name, a job he says that consists of approximately two Zoom meetings a week from one of his homes in Miami, Portugal or Monaco. He now has a net worth of £500 million, yet when he was at school in the 1950s his teachers wrote him off.

'They just thought I was stupid. There were something like forty children in the class and they couldn't cope with any child that was different. But I knew I wasn't stupid. Even when they gave us quite complicated sums, I'd always get the answer right, but I could never show them how I'd worked it out. I added up things in a different way to how we were taught. I always had the right answer at the bottom, but the bits in between were a muddle, and so they thought I was cheating. I suppose I could have slowed down and been more thorough, but I just knew I had the answer so I didn't see the point.'

This resonates with something I read while researching this book. Dyslexic people often don't know their times tables, but that's because they don't need to. What the rest of the population learns by rote, some dyslexics like Duncan and me calculate faster than tapping the digits into a calculator.

Duncan's dyslexia meant he didn't enjoy school. 'I hated it. I got something like seven out of a hundred on a geography test. I couldn't memorise where countries and cities were. Strange names just didn't stick.'

I experienced something similar when I took a medical qualification for a round-the-world sailing adventure. It was almost impossible for me to pass due to the scientific names of the drugs. Whoever came up with the word dyslexia – one of the most difficult words to spell and remember – must have been having a laugh. It's not a surprise that Duncan now says his dyslexia ruined his school days. He felt he got so far behind that he could never catch up and so just lost interest.

He even found making friends difficult. In his sixties, Duncan was diagnosed with prosopagnosia, or face blindness. He speculates now that part of the reason he didn't socialise was because he simply didn't recognise people. 'I was by myself a lot. It wasn't like I fell in with a bad crowd, I was just on my own.'

Duncan remembers seeing other boys in the school yard riding bikes. 'I got this idea that if I had a bike, then they'd play with me.' The problem with that plan was that his family was poor. Duncan grew up in post-war Clydebank in Scotland with six brothers and sisters. He lived in something called a 'requisition house' that had been bought by the council to house families while the area was rebuilt after World War II. The Bannatynes lived in the house with three other families, all sharing the same outside toilet. There was no bathroom, just a tin bath in front of a coal fire.

'I remember asking for an ice cream when the van came into the street and my mum said that we couldn't afford it. I asked why not, and her answer was that we were poor. I heard that answer so many times that my ambition in life was pretty simple: I just wanted to be "not poor".'

Duncan knew better than to ask his parents for a bike. What he did next was interesting to me. He decided to get a paper round and save up to buy a bike of his own.

'I went to the local newsagent and she took one look at me – a scruffy toerag from the wrong neighbourhood – and said that they didn't deliver newspapers to my street because no one wanted them. 'My mum wants a paper delivered,' I said. She told me she couldn't start a new paper round for one customer. 'How many customers do you need?' She told me she needed a hundred.'

So twelve-year-old Duncan knocked on his neighbours' doors and got a hundred names, got his paper round and saved up for his bike. I wonder what his school teachers would have thought if they'd known how much initiative he'd shown? To me, this is a classic example of dyslexic thinking. We tend to ask 'why not?' more than most people. *Why can't I do it? Why can't that happen? Why shouldn't I?* It's a great illustration of the 'explorative specialisation' that Dr Helen Taylor is researching.

By the time he left school, Duncan describes himself as 'an angry young man' with few career options. He enlisted in the Royal Navy but was dishonourably discharged four years later for attempting to throw a superior officer overboard. Having a problem with authority seems to be a common trait with some of the interviewees for this book.

After serving eight months in a military prison, Duncan drifted from job to job and lived pay cheque to pay cheque throughout his twenties. But when I pushed him on this period of his life before he started the care home business that would make his fortune, I found that his dyslexic thinking had an influence even then. For instance, he drove a taxi for a while, and realised he was only earning money when he had a passenger in the back. He couldn't drive two cars at once, but he could *own* two, so he bought another and leased it out to a friend. He eventually had six cars. He just kept pushing the boundaries of what was possible.

He also had what seems like the dullest job ever loading bread into a bakery van. He opted for night shifts because they paid time and a half. He then bought loaves wholesale from his employer and sold them door to door while everyone else was working a day shift. To make even more money on the side, Duncan bought cars at auction, fixed them up and sold them on for a profit. One day, an old ice-cream van came up for sale. Instead of repairing it and pocketing the profit, Duncan pulled out a telephone guide, the *Yellow Pages*, looked up ice-cream wholesalers and started selling ice creams from it. He grew Duncan's Super Ices into a business operating several vans and concession stalls in local parks. At no point did he think 'that's enough', he just kept on building and building.

He was making so much money that he started buying up property to rent out. This was the north-east of England in the 1980s when, unbelievable as it sounds now, terraced houses cost less than £20,000. He noticed that some landlords' adverts asked only for unemployed tenants. 'I thought, why would they want only unemployed people? It turns out that the government gave the tenants a voucher rather than cash and the voucher had to go to the landlord. That meant they never didn't pay their rent.' So Duncan started renting to unemployed people too.

Duncan was always seeing the bigger picture and spotting opportunities that others were missing. In his early thirties, he was watching the nightly news along with several million other people. One of the stories was about the Thatcher government changing how elderly care would be paid for.

'The policy was to pay £125 a week for each resident and one commentator said that some people were going to get very rich from those payments. And I thought, why shouldn't that be me? I immediately did the calculations. If I had a home with thirty residents, all paying £125 a week, that was a turnover of £3,750 a week, which was £195,000 a year. That was a lot of money back then.'

He found a plot of land, bought it and set about building a purpose-built care home with an ensuite toilet for every resident, something that was an innovation at a time when residents were often sharing rooms and using commodes. He went to his bank to get a loan and they asked him what his costs would be. There were statutory staffing requirements for residential homes, so he found out how many he would need and what the going rate was. When it came to his running costs, he used logic, something else dyslexics are known for. He counted up the number of rooms in his own house, calculated there were seven times more rooms in the proposed care home and multiplied his bills by seven to estimate the cost.

Initially, the bank turned him down because he'd included business rates in his plan. The bank manager told him that care homes didn't pay rates and therefore his sums were wrong. Even though that meant Duncan's figures were even better, the manager still turned him down. So Duncan, showing resilience, went to a second bank, changed the figures and learned from his first meeting what to say. It was the third bank that agreed to give him the money.

Getting the money was great, but of course those loans needed to be repaid, and until he could open a care home, he didn't have the income to make the payments. What Duncan did next would be way outside the comfort zone of most people. At first, he used profits from the ice-cream business to make the payments. Then he sold the houses he was renting out. Then he sold the ice-cream business. And when the next payment was due, he sold the house he and his wife were living in.

Duncan knew that the nursing home was worth more than it had cost him to build. Once it was fully operational, with that guaranteed £195,000 revenue, he could get a new loan based on the enterprise value of the business, not just on the value of the building. That gave him enough cash to buy another plot of land to build a second care home.

By the time he opened his third home, he had hired a secretary, which meant people no longer ignored his letters because of his spelling. Early in the business, Duncan was his own financial controller and accountant, but as soon as the cash flow allowed, he hired a business director.

There was a skill that Duncan had no choice but to hire right from the very beginning: nursing. Care homes are heavily regulated, and he was reliant on his new nursing manager to make sure his business complied with all the necessary regulation. 'She then hired all the nursing staff. I didn't get involved after that.' I asked him if he was good at delegating and he agreed. 'It probably helped that I didn't have a choice, because I couldn't do it myself.'

Delegation is a key skill in any successful business. An entrepreneur who tries to do everything is never going to grow their company. It stands to reason that the more comfortable you are getting other people to do the work for you, the quicker you can scale.

Of course, before you can delegate, you have to hire the people you are going to delegate to, and this is something Duncan did instinctively. 'Often within minutes of someone walking in the door I'd made my decision. Now, I've got an HR department and it takes them three months to hire someone!'

I was interested to learn that it's not just his employees he makes quick decisions about. He told me he fell in love with his wife almost instantly and they were living together after just four weeks. That really struck a chord: as on our second date, I said to my now wife, Madeleine, 'Why don't you move in for a week and see how it goes?' We have lived together ever since.

Does that mean dyslexics are impulsive risk-takers, or simply good judges of character? Certainly, the dyslexic thinkers I know always believe they can succeed at anything. For some reason, we are less afraid of rejection and more willing to fail.

Our ability to make decisions easily could also stem from the fact we tend to be impatient. Duncan told me a story about an employee who was stealing from one of his health clubs. 'My instinct was that I just wanted to punch his lights out. But I have this fantastic HR manager who is so patient, and who knows employment law inside out. There's obviously a process before you can fire someone, and she efficiently goes through that process, gathers the evidence and *then* she was able to fire him.'

It's infuriating to have to continue to employ someone you know is stealing from you, but it's better than getting sued yourself for unfair dismissal. I'm with Duncan, I just don't have the patience for that sort of thing. This lack of patience is often what drives me forward and I think it's the same for Duncan. I get bored easily and am always attracted to the next challenge. One of the facts I found interesting about dyslexic entrepreneurs is that we are far more likely to start multiple businesses than people without dyslexia. While a lot of careers advice is to go into a field you're passionate about, it's noticeable how many people in this book have started businesses in sectors they didn't have any affinity for, or skills in. Duncan's next business was founded on another rational decision about numbers.

The idea for his new venture came while Duncan was doing rehab exercises following a skiing accident. He was lying on a leg press in a gym looking up at the ceiling and started to count the ceiling tiles. He knew they were a foot square, and he calculated the total square footage of the building. He figured the construction costs for a gym couldn't be all that different from a care home, so he worked out how much it would cost to build his own. He also knew how much his membership was each month. When he asked how many members the club had, he very quickly realised how much money the owners were making. It wasn't long before he built a health club of his own.

I find Duncan's logic interesting, and his faith in numbers has allowed him to build two substantial businesses back to back. Remarkably, his initial calculations weren't that far out. He was right to be convinced these ventures couldn't fail to make money, but without his energy, commitment and determination they wouldn't have amounted to much. There's a saying in business that I like: where focus goes, energy flows, and Duncan put 100 per cent of his focus into these ventures. Often, it's not the decision that's right, it's the drive to support the decision that's crucial. When you're the CEO of two companies, you're not going to accomplish much if you can't make decisions, and this is something Duncan finds easy.

'When I put people into top management positions, sometimes I say to them that they will make mistakes, and that's OK because we all make mistakes. *I* make mistakes. I tell them that the only mistake that is unforgivable is lying about your mistake. If you come clean on your mistake, we can remedy that. It doesn't matter what it costs the company, because you had to make that decision. I've made mistakes that have lost the company money. It happens.'

I found Duncan – whose reputation in the Den is that of a fierce and tough negotiator – to be a flexible thinker whose opinion can be changed when circumstances change. Some people in business are of the 'my way or the highway' mindset, but Duncan's ability to change tack has obviously helped him prosper.

'We recently sold a beautiful hotel in Somerset. It was the best hotel we owned, but it was only making £100,000 to £150,000 a year. Then a Hong Kong-listed company offered us just over £3 million for it. That's twenty times' profit, so you sell.'

That doesn't mean he doesn't get attached to his businesses. After all, you can't work as hard as he has and not care about what happens to your company.

'I was very attached to the nursing-home business and I would never have sold that, but they changed the law on how elderly care was paid for. When the voucher system for paying housing benefit changed, it devastated my property rental business, and so the new changes made it a no-brainer to sell the care homes.'

Over the years, his business strategy has responded to events. When he built his health-club business, he made a point of owning the freehold of the buildings. But to get through the financial crisis of 2008, it made sense to sell the freeholds and lease the properties back. These days, he's set up a separate company to buy back some of those freeholds as a way of diversifying his assets and his risk.

One of the things Duncan is known for in the *Dragons' Den* is being competitive. In the first series of the show, he and fellow Dragon Peter Jones negotiated to invest in the same company. Peter agreed a 20 per cent stake. Duncan, being Duncan, wanted to outdo his rival and negotiated a 22 per cent stake, much to Peter's fury (he agreed in the end to accept 20 per cent to keep the peace). I wanted to know if he thought his competitiveness was linked to his dyslexia. 'I suppose that after school, where I couldn't be competitive,

I wanted to show I was better than people thought, so yes, maybe.'

This trait extends beyond his business life. When he's playing computer games with his son Tom, he says he always wants to beat him, but that's because Duncan's competitive with himself even when he's doing yoga. 'I always want to see how far I can stretch and if it's further than the day before. My son is twenty-one and a body builder, and I can stretch more than him because I do it every day.'

One of the most surprising things I found out when I spoke to Duncan is that, in his fifties, just before his *Dragons' Den* career took off, he trained to be an actor. He won a walk-on part in a Guy Ritchie movie at an auction and got the acting bug. Having worked flat out for twenty-five years at this point, and with the health clubs almost running themselves, he needed something new in his life and took himself off to drama school. He then auditioned for roles and landed parts in a handful of TV series.

Here, I see a classic dyslexic trait (restlessness) and a foundational entrepreneurial attribute (investing in yourself) that so often lead to success. Duncan's biggest part was in a BBC series called *Sea of Souls*. Unfortunately for him, it was aired after the first series of *Dragons' Den*. By then, he was too well known as a business tycoon to be cast in any more parts.

It was during an earlier TV show, long before the *Dragons' Den* format had been devised, that Duncan first heard about dyslexia. He had been asked to take part in a BBC series called *Mind of a Millionaire*. I don't remember it, but it sounds like a great format. Each week, a group of people – some of whom were millionaires – were set several tasks to complete together, such as building a contraption to get buckets of water across a stream from the limited materials provided. Two psychologists observed how the team worked together and had to guess which members of the group were millionaires. Participating in the show involved taking several psychometric tests, and it was during this process that Duncan finally received his diagnosis.

'There is a part of me that wishes I'd been diagnosed younger because of all the problems it caused me at school. But I love my life, and so I really would not want to change anything because maybe I wouldn't have ended up starting my businesses. I sometimes think if I'd passed more exams, I'd have qualified as an accountant and been on £150,000 a year.'

A pleasant life for sure, but not nearly as nice as the one he's enjoying now.

INSIGHTS FROM DR HELEN TAYLOR

Dyslexia and maths

Like Duncan, around 60 per cent of individuals with dyslexia have difficulties with certain aspects of maths, such as rote learning. Kelly struggled with numbers because she couldn't visualise them and Richard (in Chapter 12) needed more time to work things out his own way. However, like the famous mathematician Benoit Mandelbrot, many dyslexics also excel in certain areas of maths.

Having a purpose may also be important. For an individual specialised to explore the unknown, they may be more motivated to learn existing knowledge when it serves a higher purpose. This was evident in Charles Dunstone (Chapter 9), who found maths much easier to pick up in the context of his business, and in Cliff (Chapter 1), who struggled to code until it was necessary.

Duncan not being able to show his workings out is typical of exploratory learners. Dyslexics excel at finding diverse ways to reach a solution; the answers can come suddenly through insights but they may encounter difficulty retracing how they got there.

Theoretical physicist Richard Feynman worked in a similar way. His biographer, and fellow physicist, Lawrence Krauss noted that Feynman's problem-solving methods didn't follow any clear chain of logic and that answers were often intuited. He would check afterwards if he was right by trying many specific examples.

This is a well-recognised maths thinking style that was termed the 'grasshopper' by author Steve Chinn, as opposed to an 'inchworm'. The former approaches problems holistically, while the inchworm approaches them step by step. Grasshoppers, like Feynman and Duncan Bannatyne, rarely document their methods and tend to calculate intuitively. They also use estimates to reach an answer in the quickest way, just as Duncan did when calculating running costs for his care home or construction costs for health clubs.

TIPS FROM JAMIE

1. Connect the dots

Dyslexic thinkers can see and understand links between disparate ideas, even when it's counterintuitive – such as unemployed people making great tenants because the government pays their rent. Can you think of an anomaly in your environment that doesn't make sense? Explore that contradiction and see if you can identify the underlying reason. Once you've figured it out, you're halfway to a new opportunity.

2. Practise mental gymnastics

I could relate to Duncan's buzzing brain while doing rehab exercises, staring at the ceiling and using the tiles to calculate a gym's size and potential profit. Mental gymnastics like this are the trademarks of dyslexic thinkers. Patterns, numbers and opportunities are everywhere; allow your brain the time and space to go through this process. Most ideas will lead to nothing, but the one that does lead to something might end up being the size of the Bannatyne empire.

CHAPTER 8

MATT KENNEDY – THE DYSLEXIC CREATIVE

BUSINESS: FOUNDER OF FUSSY
QUALIFICATIONS: DEGREE

Matt is another entrepreneur with experience of *Dragons' Den*, but unlike Duncan Bannatyne, Kelly Hoppen and Theo Paphitis, Matt went on the show to pitch – successfully – for investment.

Matt's path towards entrepreneurship was not a straight one. He dropped out of university, twice, before embarking on careers in recruitment, surveying and advertising before the Covid lockdowns gave him the opportunity to finally launch his own business. I wanted to know what had taken him so long, and if his choices had anything to do with dyslexia.

'My parents are both academics, and both linguists, so they definitely took an interest when I had difficulties reading and spelling. They moved me out of my state school in Birmingham to a private school for a year, where I had one-to-one lessons in English. When I moved back to another state school, things were better, but not by much.'

Even as a kid, Matt describes himself as an all-or-nothing personality. 'I would get obsessed, and all credit to my parents, they supported me. When I showed an interest in photography, they sent me on a course. The same with cooking. I think they realised I wasn't academic and wanted to give me other opportunities.'

While Matt struggled with English and foreign languages at school, he loved maths because he could see how it related to the real world. Unlike me, he didn't have the same problems with showing his workings out. 'I always got A's, but geography or history or any subject that required a lot of reading was pretty woeful, to be honest.'

He was never tested for dyslexia at school, despite his parents suggesting it, because he didn't want the label. 'Kids just want to fit in, don't they? Besides, I was already getting bullied because of my weight. I had lots of friends, but I think I was seen as the weakest one in my peer group and boys can be b*stards.'

He showed some entrepreneurial flair as a kid – he somehow got hold of cigars and sold them to classmates – and when he ran out of time to complete a project in Design and Technology (D&T), he came up with an innovative solution.

'D&T was my favourite class. I've already told you I was obsessive, but I would go into the lab at the weekends to finish things. I was making a pair of speakers, but ran out of time to finish both of them before I had to submit the project, so I took a photograph of one, and Photoshopped it so it looked like there was a pair.'

Faking it until you make it is a well-trodden path in the start-up world of business.

At sixteen, he went through what he calls his rebellious phase. 'I don't know if it's related to the dyslexia or not, because I wasn't diagnosed at that point, but I think it has something to do with not fitting in, so there might be a link.'

His rebellion reached a climax when he was arrested for joyriding. 'I suppose it was middle-class joyriding because I was driving my parents' car! They really made me sweat though, saying they had to decide if they were going to press charges.'

Interestingly, I did exactly the same thing. I was driving down Bethnal Green Road and my mum was in a friend's car coming the other way. Her friend said, 'Isn't that your Jamie?' Thankfully, like Matt's mum, mine didn't press charges.

University offered an opportunity for Matt to reinvent himself. He went to Bristol to study mechanical engineering, where he introduced himself to new friends as 'Kenny', as in Kennedy, rather than Matt. He had a great time, met lifelong friends – including his now wife, Becky – ran club nights he DJ'd at and got involved in the vibrant local music scene. And when he decided to lose some weight, his all-or-nothing tendencies came to the fore. He didn't just take up cycling, he trained for a ride from Land's End to John O'Groats, losing five stone in the process.

His studies? Not so much.

'As soon as I found out that the first two years of the course were pretty much all theory, I lost interest. I realise now I should have studied product design, but I couldn't draw and that made getting accepted onto a course difficult, but it was what I wanted to do.'

Demoralised at the prospect of waiting two years before he could actually start making things, Matt dropped out. He enrolled to study accounting and finance at the University of the West of England for the following term, but dropped out of that too. Having incurred two years' worth of student debt with little to show for his money, perhaps the world of work would be where he'd find his niche? He got a job in recruitment, but after six months, that also began to look shaky when his boss took him to one side and told him they were letting him go. That's quite a lot of knock-backs for a nineteen-year-old to take in quick succession, but Matt – like so many dyslexics – is nothing if not resilient.

'I got another job in recruitment and this time it took off for me. My approach was that I knew no one wanted to speak to me – no one likes cold-callers – and it's pretty demoralising when you're going through your pitch and you know the person on the other end isn't even listening, so I changed my pitch. "I know you really don't want to speak to me, but I reckon you need someone in this field, and I'm an expert in this area and I've got a CV here of someone who could transform your operation. I know you're not looking right now, but take a look and when

you are recruiting, you'll have this candidate on file."
I started to build relationships with local employers. I'd always been quite good at reading people, but I really honed that skill in recruitment.'

Recruitment is a famously competitive, commission-based industry, but Matt learned to thrive in that environment. 'Looking back, I can see it was a good fit for me. I didn't have to write reports or do any admin; it was just sending out CVs and talking to people. And when I did have to write something, it was an email. The conversational tone of emails meant I didn't have to be formal, and of course spellcheck helped enormously.'

Even though he wasn't diagnosed at this point, he had found an industry that was suited to the dyslexic skill set, but he still didn't feel that he'd found his niche. 'They used to make you put a photo of the car you wanted to buy on your desk to motivate you. It wasn't quite *Wolf of Wall Street*, but I did enjoy the money.'

However, that was about all he did enjoy. 'I used to come home with no energy. I was tired all the time and depressed. I had more money that I'd ever had before but I felt awful.'

He lasted four years in recruitment before he quit. By the age of twenty-five, he'd dropped out of uni twice and walked away from a lucrative career. He was in danger of getting himself a reputation as someone who couldn't see things through. Encouraged by his parents, Matt went to university for a third time, this time to study surveying at Oxford Brookes.

'Because this was my third attempt at uni, my parents encouraged me to get tested for dyslexia as they thought it would help. I'd had a friend at Bristol who'd done the test there, and he'd got a free Mac to help with his studies. I think my new university gave the test for free, and if you were diagnosed, you got something like £200 a term to spend on books, so I went for it.'

Matt found the test much more interesting than he'd expected. 'It was a couple of hours and I had to do things like matching different shapes, and there was a numbers test where you had to remember a string of digits. I'd always struggled to remember phone numbers, so I sensed I was being tested for the right things. There were also reading, speaking and spelling tests.'

Getting an official diagnosis was a positive thing for Matt, even though he got a PC rather than a Mac. 'Well, first, there was the £200 book allowance. I realised that I could spend the money on Amazon, show the university the receipt and then send the books back for a refund.'

The results of the test were also helpful. 'They told me that I over-indexed in certain areas, like verbal communication, and I definitely hung onto the positives they mentioned rather than the downsides.'

Those downsides – reading and spelling, most notably – meant Matt got extra time to sit exams and could use a laptop rather than writing longhand. Those changes made a real difference, and three years later Matt finally graduated and became a qualified surveyor. He moved to London to start a new career. It didn't take long before he realised it wasn't going to work out.

'I didn't fit in. Even down to going to the pub. There was a culture of pints and I'd order a gin and tonic, and they'd be like: "Ooh, you're getting a G&T". So I was eff off, I'm going to drink what I want.'

He didn't respond well to the hierarchy of the industry, where you have to move through the ranks of chartership to become a senior, then an associate after three years. Even wearing a suit every day started to grate. So, he walked away, and – literally – burned his suit.

A third career beckoned in advertising. Matt got a scholarship to the School of Communication Arts, where he learned, somewhat ironically for a dyslexic, to be a copywriter, coming up with concepts and slogans for companies to use in their advertising campaigns. When he talks about his detour into advertising, Matt's demeanour changes and his face brightens. It's really obvious that he had finally found a career he both enjoyed and excelled at. 'I'm not very good at reading or spelling. I get the letters all jumbled up. I wouldn't really say that I'm a creative writer, but I'm good at ideas and I could put those ideas into writing.'

Typically, the way ad agencies work, a copywriter is teamed up with a designer to come up with concepts to pitch to clients. Matt really enjoyed the collaborative process and for a year or two he was generating so many ideas he couldn't possibly use them all.

'At advertising school, we were taught to look for problems. It's that clichéd thing of asking your client what keeps them awake at night and then coming up with ways of solving those headaches. So I was always spotting problems and coming up with solutions, and I started writing them all down. My obsessive side came to the fore and I just generated idea after idea.'

While eating in a Japanese restaurant, he noticed how much rice was going back to the kitchen when the tables were cleared. He wondered if he could solve that problem for the restaurant. 'I'd recently heard about a new brewer in Peckham in south London specialising in sake and something just twigged. Could the brewer use the leftover rice?'

Unsurprisingly, he came up with a brand name for the imagined drink: For Goodness Sake. Matt produced a 'pitch deck', and approached the CEO of Sticks'n'Sushi via LinkedIn and did the same with the Peckham brewery. He got meetings with both of them.

'I had a great meeting with the CEO of Sticks'n'Sushi. I wasn't even pitching a business idea to him, really. I just said that I worked in advertising, I had this idea and I wanted to make it happen. There wasn't really a commercial element to it at all. He said yes in about forty-five seconds.'

Initially, Matt and his wife Becky collected the rice themselves and took it to the brewery, who did a test batch. The quality was good enough and so it became a regular transaction, but everyone quickly realised that Matt was surplus to requirements. As he puts it, they didn't need a 'random ad guy', but they did pay him a fee for the idea.

As part of his day job, Matt would often come up with ideas for products that his agency could then get the contract to advertise. His experience with the sake venture made him realise that he had the potential to make things happen without giving his ideas away. He could also earn far more than he did as a creative in the super-competitive world of advertising. At the time, he and Becky, a head teacher at an East London secondary school, were thinking of starting a family. Matt knew he had to see if he could do something significant with one of his ideas.

'I literally had a Google Doc and I went through the list. It was New Year's Eve 2019 and my dad was driving me to the station. I remember telling him 2020 would be the year I finally started my own business. He was like, yeah, OK. It was clearly something I'd talked about too often for him to take me seriously. But we registered the company on the 1st of February.'

The 'we' in this scenario was Matt and his friend Eddie Fisher, who also had a background working for creative agencies. They'd talked about doing something together for years, and decided the venture they could both commit to was refillable deodorants, even though it was an industry neither of them had any expertise in or knowledge of.

'Sustainability has always been a bit of a theme with me. I'm not a diehard environmentalist, but I try to do what

I can. The sake idea was a way of reducing waste, and when I did my dissertation for my surveying degree, it was on mechanical ventilation heat recovery systems to heat homes more efficiently.'

I see parallels here with the theme of injustice that's come up with other dyslexic entrepreneurs I've spoken to: refillable deodorant was a solution to a crime against the planet. A business that aimed to reduce plastic waste in every bathroom in the country was definitely on-brand for Matt. And the brand they came up with for the product itself was Fussy, because they were going to be fussy about every aspect of the business, from the ingredients in the product to the ink used on the packaging. But then Covid hit and the UK, as well as much of the rest of the world, went into lockdown.

'It changed everything for me. It was a big opportunity because I was able to work on Fussy without work knowing. Georgia, my design partner, asked me what was going on because instead of sending her several ideas a day, I was just saying, yep, that's great to whatever she sent over. But I couldn't tell her what I was up to.'

From a standing start, Matt and Eddie found companies that could come up with the formula for the deodorant, make the product and manufacture the packaging, mostly by reaching out to people on LinkedIn or by googling 'packaging manufacturers'. It was that straightforward. They discovered a brand doing something similar in the US, but their refills came in plastic packaging. That made no sense to them, so Fussy's innovation was to have totally plastic-free refills.

The US is often a good place to look for new business models, and Matt and Eddie took it as a good sign that someone was proving the market case for them elsewhere. They had both put £10,000 of their own money into the business, but that wasn't nearly enough to start production. Their solution was a Kickstarter campaign.

When it launched, Kickstarter was an innovative way for early-stage businesses to raise capital. Instead of getting the money from investors or banks, the funding comes from prospective customers, who pledge to buy a product before it's made in exchange for some kind of bonus, often a discount or a personalised gift. Matt and Eddie reached out to other entrepreneurs who had run successful Kickstarter campaigns and refined their pitch based on what they'd learned. Through the Kickstarter community, they found a former banker who had done the financial modelling for other start-ups.

Not only did Fussy raise over £110,000 in pledges, but they also actually executed the most successful campaign for a personal care product in Kickstarter history. Nine months after they had registered their company, Matt and Eddie quit their jobs in advertising to go full time at Fussy.

'My agency were actually really happy for me, and they had been very supportive when we did the Kickstarter. I was lucky, actually, because they could have said that I'd had the idea on their time and they therefore owned it. The executive creative director showed her boss the product, and he said it was so good we should pitch it to Procter & Gamble. I had to tell them, thank you very much, but please don't do that.'

Matt immediately ran into a problem, however. When they had done their initial business plan, they had allocated £10,000 for the tooling to make the reusable holder for the refills. 'But the company that was manufacturing them said, because of the quality of finish you want, the tooling's going to be about £80,000. Our production costs just went pop.'

With thousands of Kickstarter customers waiting for their deodorants to be delivered, Matt and Eddie realised they were going to need to raise some capital. Family and friends came up with £50,000 but they estimated they needed more. It was around about then that they got an email from *Dragons' Den*.

'They had seen our Kickstarter and they were looking for ethical brands. There was a long application, and we had to video our pitch, and it all seemed like a lot of work when there was no guarantee of making it onto the edited programme. I don't know what percentage of pitches don't make the cut, but it was high enough for us to think twice about spending so much time on the application.'

Matt asked the production team if there was a way of making sure they made it onto TV. He knew they were looking for something original, and being dyslexic, original thinking is something Matt excels at. Given that

Fussy is all about reducing waste, he suggested hiding in a wheelie bin and jumping out of it. The producer told him that would probably do it.

There was another reason why Matt was slightly reluctant to commit so much time on what was effectively a punt: Becky was now heavily pregnant. Her unwavering support has undoubtedly been a key plank of Matt's success. 'We agreed that if we got the call from the Den, then I should go, even if she was in labour.'

On the show, it's Eddie who starts the presentation and, just as planned, the Dragons got a shock when Matt popped up out of the bin. The pair had got the Dragons' attention; now their job was to get their money. 'It was filmed in lockdown, so neither of us had had a haircut. Eddie looked like Tom Hanks in *Castaway*.'

The Dragons might not have been impressed with their appearance, but they liked their pitch. 'I think that's one of the good things about working in advertising. It was our bread and butter to stand up and pitch an idea to strangers.'

They were asking for £50,000 for 5 per cent of their business. That's a very chunky valuation they were putting on their fledgling business, but because they had already had orders from Kickstarter, they had a guaranteed revenue stream and the Dragons took them seriously. They got offers from Deborah Meaden and Peter Jones, who invested £25,000 each. Getting investment had another benefit: it guaranteed that they would make the final edit. 'It was our calculation that it was really a media-for-equity deal. For a consumer product like Fussy, that amount of airtime was worth around £1 million.'

What Matt didn't tell the Dragons was that Becky had given birth two days before to their daughter, Fleur. He describes this period of his life as relentless. If advertising had honed his pitch skills, his days in recruitment had refined his cold-calling techniques, and those months used up every bit of energy and ingenuity he had. 'Eddie and I were entering competitions for funding, designing our pitch decks for investors, hammering the phones and networking investors on LinkedIn.'

For every person who took their call, there were countless others who put the phone down. One of the many competitions they entered was for investment from a beauty sector fund run by SFC Capital. 'It was the week after *Dragons' Den* and we won it. Every investor call I had was to say that we had £250,000, to avoid having your stake diluted, do you want to come in for more?' His gift of the gab meant they ended up raising £500,000.

Fussy was now able to start manufacturing and hiring the skills they would need to expand. But the business was about to lose a key player: Eddie. Matt's co-founder had a stroke after falling and hitting his head. At first, Matt took on all the work, but as it became clear that his recovery would take time, Eddie agreed to step back from the business. As is often the way, their friendship did not survive the negotiations that left Matt in sole charge of Fussy. Losing Eddie could easily have destabilised such an early-stage business, but Matt's resilience powered Fussy through a turbulent few months. That doesn't mean it didn't take its toll.

'There were a couple of times when I broke down, I just cried. I'd never had mental health problems in the past, but there was just so much weight on my shoulders. Becky had noticed a few times that my legs had started to judder before the tears came, and she would make me lie down when she saw the warning signs.'

Initially, Fussy reached consumers through Facebook and Instagram ads and customers bought directly from their website. But to build a really significant business, Matt knew he had to get Fussy in major retailers. He decided to aim big and approach the UK's biggest retailer, Tesco. It was back to LinkedIn. 'I searched for "personal-care buyer", got a name, figured out the email address and contacted them, saying I had a pitch deck and a proposal to show them.'

When she didn't reply, Matt figured he needed specialist help and contracted a sales expert one day a week for six months. Her brief was to design the proposal to take to retailers and help him pitch it. Yet again, dyslexic comfort with delegating key tasks played a part in entrepreneurial success. Towards the end of her contract, Matt had another stab at LinkedIn. He identified the boss of the buyer who had ignored him, and sent him an email with the words 'Dragon's Den' in the subject line. Mentioning that he had investment from two Dragons was enough to get him a meeting.

'I had been about to end the contract with my sales expert, but then we got the meeting with Tesco and I kept her on and she really upsold the offer with Tesco. I might have got the meeting, but she got them to take the deal. I set it up, and she put it in the net, so to speak. Normally, Tesco follow what Sainsbury's or Boots do because they are more challenger-brand focused. If it works with the other retailers, Tesco will normally put you in 200 stores. But they put us straight into 800 stores, which was a £700,000 order.'

To say it was a big deal for Fussy is an understatement. And while Matt had much to celebrate, he suddenly had an enormous order to fill. 'Thankfully, I had hired a head of operations a year earlier and we were able to pull it off. We had to cancel a scent launch we had planned, and we had to airfreight a few things. It took all the stock we had and we had to get some short-term finance, but we did it.'

Matt looks back on that deal and is prepared to take the credit for making it happen. 'You've got to back yourself, haven't you? If I hadn't hired that head of sales six months ahead, or we hadn't been retail-ready, or got our packaging designed with enough lead time, we would have missed out. You've got to believe that, if a retailer says yes, you're ready to go. If we hadn't done those things, it would have taken another two months and we would have missed the launch with Tesco.'

Matt's immediate ambitions for Fussy now centre around expansion inside the UK and Europe. When those thresholds have been crossed, he'll introduce new products that address eliminating more plastic waste from bathroom products. It might have taken Matt a long time to find his path, but he's given himself a very good chance of making sure that entrepreneurship is his final career.

INSIGHTS FROM DR HELEN TAYLOR

Idea generation

Matt is clearly exceptional at identifying problems and then generating solutions. In experimental settings, this kind of creativity is often investigated using tests of 'divergent thinking'. One example might involve being given an object, like a brick, and being asked to generate as many different hypothetical uses as possible.

Divergent thinking leads to original ideas and is related to exploration, whereas convergent thinking leads to conventional and so-called 'correct' ideas and is more related to exploitation. Although results are less consistent for children and teenagers, a recent study showed that adults with dyslexia score higher on tests of creativity than adults without dyslexia.

Making unusual connections

The connection that Matt made between two seemingly disparate pieces of information – i.e. the wasted rice in a Japanese restaurant and a story he'd heard in the news about a sake brewer – is very typical of people with dyslexia.

One study showed that students with dyslexia had a significantly higher propensity to connect ideas in unusual combinations, which might facilitate the generation of new possibilities and original solutions. Interestingly, they also found that there was a negative correlation between such connecting abilities and reading skills; the better the students were at reading, the worse they were at making unusual connections.

This ability to connect ideas in an unusual way is a central aspect of creative thinking. This is also reminiscent of Charles Dunstone (Chapter 9) when he talks about being constantly stimulated by ideas from very different realms, and making connections that other people didn't see.

TIPS FROM JAMIE

1. Be beautiful

Dyslexic thinkers often excel in arts, design and other visual fields, as demonstrated by many of the contributors in this book. Matt is no exception; his earlier work in marketing and design gave him insight into the power and value of branding. When you look at his product, you'll notice the design is more Gucci or Apple than Rexona or Sure.

This 'beauty bias' is a critical factor in decision-making. For example, good-looking people have a better success rate in employment and higher education grades, and nearly two-thirds of consumers happily admit they are more likely to buy a product with good packaging than a badly presented product offering the same solution. It's critical to recognise the importance of presentation and aesthetics. Look at how you present yourself, your projects, and your products or business. Could a makeover be due?

2. Be different

Many dyslexic thinkers are good at standing out from the crowd. Matt's application to appear on the UK's biggest business TV show was about something other than securing investment. Matt's intuition was that if he appeared on TV and was seen by millions of viewers, he would sell more products and not require investment. He switched his attention from how to ask for money to how to present in a way that meant the BBC had to include him on the broadcast show. Knowing that you only get one chance to make a first impression, he waited quietly in a garbage bin for thirty minutes, but it meant over four million viewers saw his brand. He secured investment too. What will make you stand out in a world where we are constantly competing for attention?

CHAPTER 9

SIR CHARLES DUNSTONE – THE DYSLEXIC BILLIONAIRE

BUSINESS: FOUNDER OF CARPHONE WAREHOUSE AND FIVE GUYS EUROPE
QUALIFICATIONS: A LEVELS

Sir Charles Dunstone is, without doubt, one of Britain's most successful business leaders. As the founder of Carphone Warehouse – the largest independent phone retailer in the world – he turned a £6,000 investment into a £1.8 billion company and he is now the driving force behind the high-street restaurant chain Five Guys in the UK and Europe. Not bad for a kid whose teachers told him he was lazy. Despite the troubles he encountered at school, Charles describes dyslexia as a gift.

'I wasn't very clever. I had a good time at school and had lots of friends. I was probably a bit anti-establishment and did things that should have got me in trouble. I didn't let academic work bother me too much because I just didn't care. Weirdly, if I had to take a chemistry O level now, I would probably find it quite interesting, but at the time it was just boring, and irrelevant. I couldn't pay attention and it didn't go in. I find it very hard to focus on something I'm not interested

in. The trouble with being at school was that 90 per cent
of it was not interesting.'

Dyslexia wasn't a word he heard during his childhood
– he was born in 1964, so was at school before dyslexia
entered mainstream consciousness – and that meant
there wasn't any extra help for him, even with the
additional resources at his exclusive private fee-paying
school. 'The teachers just thought I was lazy. In those
days, people thought that if you just put a bit more effort
into it, you could do better.'

His dad was an executive for the oil giant BP and was
sent abroad, which meant Charles boarded from the
age of thirteen, which he loved for two reasons. 'The
good thing if you're lazy is if you go to boarding school,
no one's really on your back. I had a lot of friends who I
got into modest amounts of trouble with. Smoking and
those sorts of things. I was with a crowd of people that
were all trying to challenge things. I guess I was always
trying to challenge the establishment. I wasn't rude
or confrontational. I wasn't fighting the system; I was
subverting it.'

His nickname at school, according to his mate and
future TV and radio presenter Johnny Vaughan, was
Stubber after the cigarettes he smoked out of sight of the
teachers. Charles's desire, and ability, to challenge the
establishment played a part in his first business, which he
started, aged fourteen or fifteen, with a school friend.

'We sold what were called "fancy goods", things like
photochromatic sunglasses, pens, lighters, that sort of

stuff, that we bought out of *Exchange and Mart*. I was quite savvy, I bought one of everything and then we created a bit of a stir because everyone wanted this stuff and we'd say, "Oh, very sorry, I'm afraid that's so popular we sold out. But don't worry, we've got more coming Tuesday, so I'll order one for you." We were very simple-minded: if we bought something for £2, we sold it for £4, and when you said you wanted something, we took a 50 per cent deposit. So, we got all the money in to buy the goods, and then as we handed them out, we collected the profit. It was a sweet business.'

Johnny Vaughan was one of Charles's salesmen and anyone who's seen Johnny on TV or heard him on the radio won't be surprised to hear he was brilliant at it. As with most things in life and business, if you do something you love, you tend to be very good at it. I asked Charles if he shared Johnny's flare.

'He's such a performer, Johnny. I think he was more interested in the chat than actually being a salesman. I'm not very good at the hard sell, not a very aggressive salesman, but quite good at making a relationship and understanding what people want. I think I had quite good EQ.'

In a real sign of his flair for a good deal, Charles sold the business before he left the school. 'With immaculate timing, when the school had bought all of this stuff that there was to buy, we actually managed to sell the business to a couple of other lads in the school, so we got the final lick of the spoon.'

After sitting his A levels, Charles got a place at university, but his interest in business meant he went into the world of work. 'I got a job through my grandfather. He knew someone who put me in touch with a business in Cambridge that sold personal computers, which was all to do with the BBC Micro at the time. I worked there as a salesman, selling to companies who were going to sell them on again. Then I got a job with NEC, a Japanese technology company, selling computers, and from there I got transferred within NEC to sell mobile phones. It was right in the beginning of the early days of mobile phones, and it was like, wow, this is an amazing business. It was a technological revolution that gave people freedom.'

Charles often travelled to Japan for meetings and got to see a totally different business culture. 'This would have been 1987, 1988, when Japan was ruling the world. I used to sit in these meetings and go, "My God, if these people are ruling the world, everyone else must be really terrible." The Japanese way was very, very slow, and people were dropping off to sleep in the meeting, and there were hundreds of people at these big tables.'

NEC's clients were businesses like Vodafone and Cellnet, who then sold the phone to customers and did the billing. 'It was an interesting entrepreneurial time. The guy who was already there kept BT and Vodaphone and the big accounts, and because I was new, I got given the smaller, more janky, accounts. But, actually, it was my janky guys who grew the most, and did the most business, because it was a who-dares-wins buccaneering market at the time, and that was fascinating. This was the time of Thatcher, free enterprise and the yuppie. The mobile phone became a real mark of the freedom of Thatcherism and the 1980s go-getters.'

Working alongside these disruptors had a massive impact on Charles. NEC was selling phones to other businesses, who in turn often focused on staff-wide contracts at other big firms. It seems like another world now, but in the mid-1980s mobile phones were the size of suitcases. In fact, they were so big that they were mostly fitted into cars as they were too large to carry around. Charles realised the opportunity was selling to individuals.

'The people who benefitted from mobile phones the most weren't people who worked for large organisations, it was the self-employed and the small businesses. My idea was to say, OK we could normalise mobile phones and specialise in helping people who don't have a procurement department.'

Charles set up his new business, aged twenty-five, using £6,000 in savings to get things off the ground. Remarkably, this would be the only investment anyone would ever make in the company before it floated eleven years later for £1.8 billion.

'It was a bit of a dubious industry back then; it was all a bit under the railway arches and not very customer-friendly. We started in a flat on the Marylebone Road. And a friend who was a music producer had the master bedroom and the spare room, and we had the sitting room and the dining room. We put loads of phones in, which we bought from the companies I used to sell to when I worked at NEC, stuck some adverts on Capital Radio that we couldn't have afforded if it hadn't worked out, and waited for the phone to ring. It went mad for seven minutes after the ad aired, and then we waited until the next ad.'

Back then, mobile phones weren't just new, they were confusing. 'We'd sign the customer up on the phone and then send someone out to fit the phone in someone's car or deliver the portable. Initially, we called ourselves Professional Cellular Services, but when we started placing ads in the *Evening Standard*, we realised we needed a name that was about what we do, that gave the idea of value and price. We wanted to give the impression that you were buying direct from the distributor or warehouse, something that said big and cheap, because at the time the killer retailers were the big-format discounters like Toys R Us.'

His sister designed the original Carphone Warehouse logo, not because she had any professional design qualifications, but because she was available. 'It was very hand to mouth. We were so young and didn't know any better. We were just full of enthusiasm, a can-do attitude and thought we'll just make it up as we go along.'

The fledgling business was soon evicted from the Marylebone flat because they were running it without planning consent, and they moved into a derelict shop down the road. Initially, they used it as an office, then opened it as a shop when they had made enough money. Within three years they had twenty shops, and then acquired another eighteen from the receivers dealing with a high-street chain that had gone bust. When it came to the corporate governance side of the business, Charles hired an accountant to deal with Companies House and file their accounts. Now that the figures were about money rather than abstract numbers, his brain found it easier to engage with a subject he'd struggled with at school. 'It took me three goes to get maths O Level, but I could really understand the maths when it was about my margin, or what my rent bill was.'

The company made a loss on every handset it sold, but it made a fortune in the fees it received from the service providers, short-lived companies like Mercury and Orange that have since been merged into the handful of networks operating in the UK today. The competition between the service providers was so fierce that they incentivised Charles to sign his retail customers to their contracts.

'The hardware was subsidised by the activation bonus. We bought the phone for £200 and charged the customer £100, which was less than they could buy it for themselves. In the end, we often gave them the phones for free. But we got paid £500 from the service provider for activating the line. The customer thought it was unbelievable because we'd come and fit a phone for £100, but we were making three or four hundred quid.'

This sounds great, but cash flow was a concern as they had to juggle the payment terms on the phones they bought – usually thirty days – and wouldn't get the money from the service providers until after contracts had been signed. Nevertheless, they successfully juggled and never needed to apply for outside loans or pitch to investors for cash.

Charles very modestly says that it would have been hard not to have made money selling mobile phones in those days as it was such a growth industry, but you don't subsequently become the biggest independent retailer of mobile phones without considerable acumen to go with your luck. You can get lucky with the right time and the right place, but you still need the right person to do the job. Carphone Warehouse's success came down to Charles's dedication to their level of customer service.

'It was all very new and quite complicated, and coverage was patchy. A customer would come in and say I live in Chelmsford, I drive here every day, which network should I be on? We'd work it all out for them. We'd give you the most cost-effective service and a phone that did what you needed it to on a network that was going to have the best coverage for where you used it. And then you just didn't need to worry about it; we took care of it. We were so single-mindedly focused on the customer that we didn't pay our people commission to sell one network or service over another. It really was impartial, and that became a sort of religion in the business. Customers really did trust us more than anyone else.'

Mobile telephony was such a frenzied market, and there was so much competition between the service providers in those early days, that the industry attracted a fair percentage of sharks.

'It was all slightly dodgy. At the Mobile News Awards, which were the industry awards held every year at the Hilton on Park Lane, there was a stabbing one year. We tried to keep out of the worst of it. People used to smash each other's shops up. There was a guy who had to go to America because he fell out with some people from Ireland who threatened to put AIDS-infected needles in his children. It was quite gruesome at times, and quite rough, but we were seen as public schoolboys who were better presented and a bit more courteous and honest.'

Everyone wanted growth, and the service providers were throwing money around to make sure they came out on top. Charles made plenty of money himself but says he could have made more.

'It always made a profit, but it probably took three years until I thought, "Wow, this thing might not go bust." I realised that it could actually be enduring and had a brand that meant people came to us not just because they had heard an ad on Capital Radio. But, actually, we were the busy fools, because while we might have been making a few hundred quid, the service providers were making thousands from each contract. There was a lot of money sloshing around. I went to the industry awards in the US, and in the car park outside it was like a supercar showroom.'

When Carphone Warehouse re-signed customers, they got another bonus and they eventually ended up with 35 per cent of the UK market. 'The UK had among the cheapest mobile phone running costs of any country. My contacts at the networks told me that it was my fault, because we came in and played everyone off against each other to get the best deals for our customers. If a service provider said they weren't getting enough business, we told them they needed to put in an incentive.'

At the time, Charles was so focused on delivering the best for his customers that he didn't realise they had inadvertently created another opportunity. 'What's so annoying is we were Compare the Market, but we never understood that you could do those comparisons for something other than mobile phones.'

Eleven years after Charles left NEC, he floated Carphone Warehouse on the London Stock Exchange. The company wanted to expand into domestic telephony and needed some capital to do that.

'I also wanted to take a bit of money off the table, and really the only way you could do that, and still have control and run it, was to go public. If we'd taken private equity, an investor would have needed an exit.'

When the brokerage handling the flotation looked at the business, they were stumped because it had never taken on board any capital investment since Charles's initial £6,000. 'They looked at the paid-up share capital and thought there was an error. They'd never seen a business that'd had an infinite return on capital. We didn't have any debt either.'

He found the process of flotation a bruising experience. 'Because you've never done it before, it's very time-consuming and very hard work. You suddenly have all these other people commenting on and judging your business that you're extremely protective of. It was a growing-up moment, definitely.'

With the cash injection came new responsibilities. 'You definitely take on more burden, because you have to do the half-yearly reporting, you're seeing shareholders, you've got a lot of other people interested in your business then.' Added paperwork is not something a dyslexic person looks forward to. 'I don't remember feeling that I was struggling. You just had to do it. But because it's your business and you care about it, you've got the focus to be able to handle it.'

With the new investment on board, in 2003 Carphone Warehouse set up TalkTalk, which provided old-fashioned landlines to customers' homes. The growth in the demand for broadband was astonishing, and the new business was demerged from the parent company. Both companies subsequently grew through acquisitions and mergers. In 2016, Charles sold Carphone Warehouse to the electronics retail giant Dixons and took up the position of chair. He finally left the company he had founded two years later after misgivings about the direction of the business.

'I will never be in any business that I think is exploitative, that does gambling or consumer credit, because all of those are about the exploitation of the most vulnerable in society. The new chief executive came from a venture that had a strategy that I felt was about tricking people into taking contracts and ripping them off. I saw that could end up being the strategy at Carphone Warehouse too, so I was like, I'm out. I had travelled around the country perhaps more than the average person to visit our shops, and you see the deprivation, and you see the poverty, and you see all the betting shops are in the poorest neighbourhoods, and I could see what was happening and just thought: this is exploitation.'

It's another demonstration of the link between dyslexia and injustice. Charles went back to TalkTalk full time and started to sell his shares in Carphone Warehouse.

Charles is still the executive chairman of TalkTalk but also, through a joint venture with former Carphone Warehouse CEO Roger Taylor, he now invests in promising brands with the potential to disrupt. Those brands include Boxpark, Me+Em, the womenswear brand, Purple Bricks, the online estate agency, and high-street restaurant chain Five Guys Europe.

Five Guys is a fast casual burger chain that started in the US, where it had over a thousand restaurants. Knowing it was a good brand and a good business, Charles cold-called the owners to talk about overseas expansion. They set up a 50:50 joint venture to take the business into Europe and they now have over three hundred restaurants in the UK, Germany, France, Spain and Portugal and are opening another thirty or so a year.

'It is a phenomenal business. And it's also a beautiful business because everything else sometimes is so complicated. Five Guys is so pure. You're hungry, you come to us, we cook you some food, you give us money, you eat the food. It's all done so simply. There's no Apple, there's no Vodaphone, there's no BT, there's just food ingredients. Coke is the largest organisation that we deal with, and they only want to sell more Coke. It's refreshingly simple and straightforward. People have been feeding one another for thousands and thousands of years; it's not complicated.'

Charles and his team didn't completely replicate the US model. In the US, Five Guys tended to be in malls, but the European branches are all in prime locations, and that allowed them to do something quite remarkable: Five Guys has never advertised in Europe.

'It's the power of the sites. We've always said no PR, and our rule is that we've only got one chance to advertise and that's done on site. We want customers to visit because they've chosen to go there, and not advertising is weirdly part of the success of the brand because it's so authentic. Everyone that's gone to Five Guys has gone because they feel they've discovered it. Even in the restaurants, the pictures are of reviews that other people have made of Five Guys. Five Guys will never talk about itself.'

The success of Five Guys, like Carphone Warehouse, is down to Charles's focus on his customers, which I'm going to attribute partly to his dyslexia and his enhanced powers of empathy. 'I think most shops are run with the proprietors stood in the stockroom door looking at the shop, but you have to run a business from the pavement looking into the shop. Some people find that incredibly difficult to do.'

That dyslexic ability to put himself in other people's shoes has brought Charles phenomenal success. I was intrigued to find out if he thought dyslexia had any negative impact on how he operates.

'Well, if I type anything, there's a lot of wiggly red lines. One of my worst things used to be if I wrote "Carphone Warehouse", I'd always write "Craphone Warehouse"! I can't spot errors in what I've written because I always read what I meant, not what I've written. I'm better at spotting mistakes in other people's work, though. I've also noticed recently that I run words into each other. So, if I was going to write, say, "different" and then "entertainment", I'd run them together because one ends with "-ent" and the next word starts with it. I think that's because my brain is going faster than I can write. If you gave me algebra, obviously, I wouldn't have a clue. But anything to do with percentages, I've got. I'm very quick to add up, though I find I get my decimal points muddled up, which can be embarrassing. But if you go, what's 70 per cent of a certain figure, I'll work that out roughly very quickly. I'm very numerate in that sense, but only in quite a thin range of competence.'

It's at this point in our interview that Charles says he needs to step out to present a birthday cake to one of his team. I thought about how special that team member would feel that the chair of the business, a man who has founded two billion-pound ventures, was taking the time to sing happy birthday. It was another illustration of how dyslexic leaders have the emotional intelligence to make sure their people are taken care of and feel valued.

When we continued our conversation, he told me he still experiences the same frustrations he did in those Japanese board meetings at the beginning of his career.

'I think it's the dyslexic in me that means I don't have the discipline to slow down. Quite often I have to play Tetris, or something, in a meeting because people go so slowly that I can't concentrate on it unless I've also got something else to do. I hear everything, I really do, and they all think I'm not listening, but I know exactly what's going on. Without it, you'd actually stop listening because your mind goes off somewhere else. You need a focus.'

Unsurprisingly, Charles has no plans to retire. After struggling at school because of a lack of interest, the problem now is switching off. 'The friction that has to be overcome is what made me. There's a lovely expression from one of our guys who's been working with me for years. He said you must remember that work is the rent that you pay to live, and I think that's a really good expression. You just need to keep the brain going, worry about things, and get excited about things. Working with different management teams, some of them are giving us good news, some are giving bad news, but together we work on it, we laugh, we construct it, we come up with ideas, we do stuff. It's very fulfilling.'

INSIGHTS FROM DR HELEN TAYLOR

Challenging the status quo

Charles's anti-establishment sentiments question the status quo, aligning him with what we'd expect from an exploratory approach. Continually questioning existing knowledge is extremely important because amid changes in the environment and knowledge, it is crucial to filter out the obsolete and prioritise the relevant. You can think of it like testing the foundations: you want to make sure the basis of how you do things is solid in order to move forward. This mechanism leads to improvements and potentially fosters innovation, which is another reason dyslexic individuals are good at business.

Research indicates that, in general, children tend to be more exploratory. While some grow up to become better at more local exploration or exploitation, it seems that dyslexic individuals continue to be global explorers, becoming more capable with experience.

Customer focus and perspective-taking

Charles is exceptionally customer-focused and good at perspective-taking, behaviour that seems to be typical of dyslexic entrepreneurs. They seek to develop a deep understanding of customer needs and then problem-solve accordingly. As Charles said, 'You have to run a business from the pavement looking into the shop, and people find that incredibly difficult to do.'

Why do dyslexics find it easier? We need more research, but tantalising clues exist. For example, studies have demonstrated that children with dyslexia have heightened emotional sensitivity. A more global exploratory bias would also suggest that dyslexics build more 'global' or multi-dimensional internal models to understand the world, something we see borne out in these interviews. These factors likely play an important role in the dyslexic aptitude for perspective-taking in different contexts.

TIPS FROM JAMIE

1. Be empathetic

One of the well-known traits of dyslexia is increased levels of empathy. Charles's ability to put himself in customers' shoes is an excellent example. Make some time to put yourself in another person's shoes. Be your customer for a day, partner for an hour or boss for the length of a meeting. Write down how that makes you feel. What perspective does this bring?

2. Be yourself

Charles realised that being a public schoolboy in the mobile phone sales environment meant people were more likely to trust him over others, and he used this to his advantage. Dyslexic thinkers are good at recognising and playing to their strengths. Document who you are, your talents and your main strengths against the environment you want to improve within. What's unique about you, and how will you use that to your advantage?

3. Focus intensely

I loved Charles's anecdote about playing Tetris in meetings. If your brain struggles to concentrate, try giving it something to do. Doodling, squeezing a stress ball or plaiting your hair help settle your mind and enable you to maintain intense focus.

CHAPTER 10

PHILLI ARMITAGE-MATTIN — THE DYSLEXIC CHEF

BUSINESS: FOUNDER OF CHEFPHILLI
QUALIFICATIONS: MASTER'S DEGREE

Philli Armitage-Mattin is best known as 'Chef Philli', a finalist on the 2020 series of *MasterChef* and author of *Taste Kitchen Asia*, a recipe book with a dyslexic difference. Instead of telling readers to follow her recipes to the milligram, she encourages them to adjust the meals to suit their own tastes and she uses pie charts and graphs to help them explore flavours.

I was surprised to learn that Philli didn't grow up in a foodie house, and as a kid she couldn't get enough of potato cakes with smiley faces swimming in a plate of ketchup. It wouldn't be until her twenties that she found that food was something she had both a talent, and a passion for, and that's probably because as an A* student, great things were expected of her academically. In fact, she was so bright, no one believed she had dyslexia.

'Anything creative and anything maths or science, I'd absolutely fly at. I can see a page of algebra and be like, yes, cool. And any of those competency questions where you have to find the next thing in the sequence, I'm absolutely great at those. I loved all of that. But anything with comprehension or reading, I was so sick. But I was awful at English. I hated it. Reading out loud put the fear of God in me.'

Despite having an older brother who was dyslexic, Philli's mum refused to believe that she had a problem. She wonders now if gender played a role, although there is no evidence that dyslexia affects girls less than boys.

'I feel like, in boys generally, it's a little bit more accepted than girls, and so I had to hide it. Or at least not show it as much. My handwriting's a bit neater, and girls don't mess around in school as much. I was in the gifted and talented stream for maths, but had to stay behind and was in the lowest set for reading and English. I said to my mum I thought I was dyslexic. She said, '"Oh, Phillipa, don't be stupid, you're not." I was hurt by it, I didn't want to be called stupid, but I now think that if my mum hadn't said that, I wouldn't have developed different skills to make me be able to pass exams.'

Because she wasn't disruptive, or a cause for concern, Philli was the only one worried about her difficulties with English. Eventually, she got some tutoring, but the only thing that made a difference was time.

'When I'm reading a page, I'll have to read it and read it and read it. I need to read it three times before it'll go in my brain. In class, I couldn't keep up. I've never read a book – I've written one, but I've never read one – but I do listen to them.'

Not only does Philli use services like Audible and Speechify to absorb the written word more effectively, she has discovered that she can listen to things at double speed and still take it all in.

'Plus, I can multi-task. I can cook or do ironing or send emails at the same time. When I listen to something, I'm like, it's in, done, and I'll remember it. If I'd known that at an earlier stage, it would have made a difference.'

It's certainly something I hope academics and politicians make a note of, especially as services like Speechify (see Chapter 1 on Cliff Weitzman) make it possible to create audio versions of all types of written content.

After school, Philli went to university to study for an integrated master's degree in chemistry. She thought she'd probably go on to become a management consultant like many of her peers, but a series of events changed the direction of her life. First, it turned out that her professor had also tutored Heston Blumenthal (another dyslexic thinker), a chef whose restaurants and TV shows were gaining a reputation for pushing the boundaries of flavour through molecular gastronomy (bacon ice cream, anyone?). Philli was a huge fan of Heston's and now paid even more attention to her professor's tutorials on the molecular chemistry of food. She also found she was interested in the psychology of food, a subject that incorporates elements like memory and culture into why we like certain types of food.

'I contacted this amazing professor, Charles Spence, at Oxford who does food psychology. I wanted to read everything he'd written. I would ask him questions, and he'd send me some papers, and that's when my dyslexia kicked in because I was like, this is so much text I need to read. In my last year at uni I just needed more time to read everything, so I asked to be tested for dyslexia as I needed more time in the exam. My lecturers agreed and when the results came back, I was off the charts.'

At this stage, Philli was an enthusiastic amateur cook who enjoyed making meals for friends; she wasn't considering it as a career. She became friends with a girl studying psychology who was really into interior design. Together they decided to put on pop-up restaurant nights where Philli stretched her skills to cook twenty covers a night. 'We were part of an entrepreneurial class where you were put with other people who wanted to do entrepreneurial stuff. It was really fun and I learned that you can design jobs that are perfect for you.'

As part of her interest in the psychology of food, Philli also started to pay attention not just to how a meal tasted but what it looked like, and even how it sounded. How a meal is visually presented on a plate also makes a huge difference, and the perfect meal will provide a balance of textures and flavours. As a dyslexic, this balancing of the senses played a big part in how Philli created menus. It's reminiscent of how Kelly Hoppen (see Chapter 2) talked about using all the senses in her interior designs. 'All the senses matter. You've got your olfactory response, but the crunch of food matters too. Your ears conduct sound and that tells you something important about what you're eating.'

Philli still didn't think she'd build a career around food. Her light-bulb moment came when her dad took her to L'Enclume, a three Michelin star restaurant in the Lake District near where her grandparents lived.

'I thought chefs were like rock stars and I was enthralled by the team there, working like dancers and producing this amazing food. I mentioned that I loved food and was studying chemistry, and they invited me to see their development kitchen.'

L'Enclume was one of the first restaurants in the country to use food it grows, and rears, on its own farm, and their approach to developing menus was methodical and experimental. It was here that Philli realised she could have a career in the food industry that used her chemistry to create flavour and her passion to feed people.

She recognised that cooking for twenty people in a pop-up restaurant wasn't going to cut it in the brutal restaurant industry, so she applied for, and got, a coveted apprenticeship with Gordon Ramsay's restaurants.

'You're like a machine as an apprentice. There's no creativity, you're just doing what you're told. For me, it was a means to an end and I wanted to get in and out of that kitchen in the shortest time possible. I learned a lot, but it was really tough.'

Eighteen-hour days, six days a week. It wasn't just the hours and the combative kitchen environment that Philli found hard, it was the lack of creativity. So when she qualified, she looked around for different opportunities.

She got a job in a development kitchen producing ready meals for supermarkets, something she found incredibly rewarding. Devising recipes that have to conform to government health guidelines, customer expectations of convenience and supermarket profit margins was a challenge she enjoyed. And then her career took another turn. 'I got drafted into a French/Japanese restaurant and it was the first time I ever tasted miso, and I was like, what is this paste and how can it add so much flavour?' It was the start of an obsession with Asian food. Most people assume that because her mum is of Indian heritage, Philli learned to cook at home. In truth, the curries in their household came in the form of takeaways (although to save money, her mum did cook the rice and chapatis herself).

Unlike most people who might have bought a recipe book to learn more about their new passion for Asian food, Philli instead bought a one-way ticket to Tokyo. 'I mean, I emailed people first. I spoke to suppliers in London who delivered our wagyu beef and asked for introductions. My parents thought I was crazy, but I was like, I just want to eat, I want to cook, I want to taste.'

It's another example – and we've seen plenty in this book – of a dyslexic brain getting locked onto a subject and jumping in feet first for a total immersive experience. A few months later, Philli gave up her steady development kitchen job – a rare catering gig that didn't involve the eighteen-hour days or the constant pressure of restaurant cooking – and touched down in Tokyo.

Despite not speaking a word of Japanese, Philli worked in kitchens across Japan, including the renowned Den restaurant. She then travelled to China to develop her understanding of flavour and spice on what became a ten-month odyssey. She came back to the UK with notebooks full of ideas, but because she's dyslexic, these notebooks didn't contain any words.

'It's just pictures, drawings and illustrations of recipes. If you give me three ingredients now, I'll draw out a dish, I'll create the whole recipe and I'll know exactly how I'm going to cook it, how it's going to be plated, the colours, everything.'

Almost always, the dish Philli has imagined in her head, or sketched in her notebook, will end up exactly as she had envisaged. 'Sometimes, and it'll be really frustrating for me, I'll be like, it hasn't quite worked. Let's think about this, and it'll take iterations. Sometimes, I wake up in the middle of the night and I'll think of a dish and even without practising it, it'll be cool.'

Unlike other chefs who might create dishes based on elements like protein, carbohydrate and vegetables, Philli balances recipes around what she describes as six essential palates – salt, sweet, tart, fat, spice and herb. Each of us will like these flavours in different amounts, and finding the food we love is about finding a balance between these palates.

Although Philli knew she had found her passion, she wasn't sure how she could make a career in the hierarchical restaurant industry. She didn't enjoy the 'yes, Chef' culture of high-pressure kitchens where there was no room for creativity, and as a young woman the macho environment could be particularly stressful. She went back into development kitchens, and while this indulged her science brain, her entrepreneurial and creative side had little outlet. That was satisfied by working as a restaurant consultant.

'I would take someone's idea and turn it into an actual concept. Maybe someone's got a lease to a property and an idea for a restaurant, but I can turn it into an actual functioning restaurant. They may have an idea of how they want their kitchen designed, but is it going to flow? I look into the trends of today. What's the feel going to be? What glassware and crockery are they going to use? How are the customers going to flow? What's the feel of the place? What payment system are they going to use? Are they going to do delivery? What are their streams of revenue? What supply chain are they going to use to get their ingredients in? I will write the menu and do a full training manual where you get to learn each of the dishes. I'll do the nutritionals.'

Nutritionals is a relatively new concern for restaurant chains now that businesses of a certain size are legally required to list the calorific content of their meals on their menus. Philli's clients for her consultancy work range from individual restaurants to Krispy Kreme donuts. This sounds to me like a great way to occupy a dyslexic brain, but for Philli it meant she wasn't getting to exploit her passion for Asian flavours.

Having grown in confidence on her tour of Asia, Philli auditioned for *MasterChef: The Professionals*, one of the highest-rated cookery programmes on UK television, partly because having a regular job meant she was not busy enough. Like a lot of dyslexics, she finds not being busy very stressful. Philli made it through several auditions and filming started just as the world went into lockdown in the spring of 2020.

'I had to learn a load of recipes – for example, an anglaise or a basic ice cream or a sorbet base. Memorising things for the short term is really, really difficult for me. So my partner Tom, who is also dyslexic, came up with a way of representing the menus visually, like a pie chart, so I didn't have to remember exact numbers, just the ratios.'

Having that image in her head meant she could recall an entire recipe, even in the stressful and competitive environment of the *MasterChef* studio. She rehearsed as many dishes as she could – she once cooked six ducks in a day that Tom had to taste – but one of the challenges on *MasterChef* is cooking a meal with a list of ingredients chosen by the judges. She tried to prepare for this too: Tom would come home with random ingredients and put her on the spot to create something.

Where the rest of us might need to consult several recipe books to come up with a meal, Philli's brain immediately imagines the dish those ingredients could become. All the practising worked: Philli made it through to the final, although she didn't win the series.

Looking back, she thinks that may have been to her advantage. 'I think if you win, you might just sit on your laurels, but I've kept pushing.'

MasterChef opened many doors for Philli and enabled her to get an agent. One of the best things about having an agent is that Philli – who dislikes confrontation – now has someone to negotiate contracts on her behalf. Some of those negotiations are with top London hotels where Philli often does short-term residencies. One such residency – at the InterContinental – came about because she impressed *MasterChef* judge Marcus Wareing so much that he recommended her for it.

For three months, Philli led the InterContinental team, who produced menus to her specifications. She also got involved with the design of the restaurant for the duration of her residency, down to the flower displays.

'*MasterChef* gave me credibility, but in those situations I almost always feel like an imposter because I haven't earned my stripes. But at the same time, I'm here, and I'm doing it and it works. Sometimes I feel confident, and sometimes I feel unsure. It goes two ways.'

One of her residencies was at a Japanese restaurant, and the menu started with a questionnaire for guests. She describes it as being similar to the flow charts they used to do in *Smash Hits*. 'If you like this, then you'll like that.' At the end of the chart were six different butters that corresponded to the six different palates. Diners would receive the butter they liked the best served with their shokupan bread rolls.

I can see that taking part in a series of residencies is perfect for a dyslexic chef, as every few months you move on to another exciting project, but that does mean she doesn't get to be her own boss. Philli seems OK with that.

'People keep asking me when I'm going to start my own restaurant, but if I do that, suddenly it becomes my problem if the fridge breaks down or there's a leak. I hate structuring my day. My calendar stresses me out because I'm not doing all the things, and then I feel I'm not being productive, and it's stressful.'

Like a lot of other dyslexics, she has plenty of enthusiasm at the beginning of projects – when her explorative brain is firing on all cylinders – but can run out of steam towards the end when more exploitative tasks are required to get something over the line. It sounds to me that Philli could team up with a non-dyslexic business partner, but she says one of the things she struggles with is delegation.

'I find that really hard. I find it hard to explain what I'm trying to get at. I did let go of my social media for a while, just because it was giving me a lot of anxiety. But it ended up being more work because I'd have to check and make sure that it sounded like my tone of voice. So I was like, I'll just do it myself; it's mine anyway. If I've got a time limit, I can do a month's work in a day and it'll be absolutely fun, and I'm really good at focusing on new projects.'

Creating recipes and sharing tips on Instagram is a big part of Philli's working week these days, as well as a lucrative source of income, as brands pay her to use their products.

It helps that she likes presenting and the technology means Philli can do everything herself without needing to delegate.

'It sounds a bit weird, but I enjoy being in front of a camera. You can just do it on your phone and the apps make it so easy. I get to do everything from creating the recipes to the shooting and editing, and I find that very stress-relieving. Occasionally, one day of work on Instagram can make more money than three months of work at the restaurant, and I'm like, what's the sense in this?'

One of Philli's post-*MasterChef* projects has been her book, *Taste Kitchen Asia*. And her reluctance to delegate came to the fore again during production. She wanted to do it all, partly because they had a tight budget, and partly because she wanted to have control. In the end, she let a professional photographer take the shots, but she insisted on styling the shoots.

Thousands of Asian cookery books have been published, but because Philli takes a different approach – and I'd argue it's a dyslexic approach – her book stands out from the crowd. Even on TV, where you can see steam rise and hear a steak sizzle, it's difficult for a viewer to know what a dish will taste like. That's even more true with books, when you can only see a static image. Philli wanted to find a way to communicate what a dish would taste like to a reader so that they wouldn't waste their time cooking a dish they wouldn't like. 'I thought, OK, I need to depict flavour. How do I show that? As a graph? As an image? I felt like home cooks don't taste enough as they're cooking. So, I wanted to encourage people to taste and adjust.'

The answer was an extension of the pie charts Tom developed for Philli to memorise her *MasterChef* dishes. Her 'flavour wheels' are colour-coded and each colour corresponds to one of the six palates, so you can instantly look at a recipe and understand the balance between salt, sugar, fat, etc. The size of each slice varies according to the main flavour of the dish.

But the great thing about Philli's recipes is that once you've learned what your particular palate profile is, you can adjust her recipes to suit your personal taste. This seems to me to be a dyslexic innovation.

These days, Philli is taking a bit of time to explore what to do next. Does she start her own ready-meal brand, open a restaurant or see where her media career takes her? In between meetings and planning sessions, she often mentors younger chefs and gives demonstrations at industry events. She enjoys the public-facing aspect of her work, just so long as she doesn't have to memorise a script.

'I hate that. If I can get it down to a few bullet points and then go off script, I'm OK, but if I have to memorise it word for word, I'm like, no. If I'm given a big piece of text, I'll use Speechify and listen to it.'

She also uses voice notes rather than writing emails because she can speak so much better than she can write. She rarely writes longhand because her hand can't keep up with her brain.

Like the other interviewees, Philli has learned to embrace her dyslexia. 'At the beginning of my career, I was upset that I had dyslexia and now I'm proud, I'm happy I've got it and I do think it's a superpower. If I didn't have it, I wouldn't be where I am today.'

INSIGHTS FROM DR HELEN TAYLOR

Interdisciplinary/systems approach

People with dyslexia tend to work across disciplines, as we saw with Philli's studies. They don't specialise narrowly in depth (which is closer to exploitation) and don't see the same subject boundaries others do. By exploring broadly, dyslexics develop a more networked understanding; a complex systems-level approach. This is in line with global exploratory learning and a need to understand any issue holistically by examining it from many different perspectives. This can give them a greater thoroughness of understanding, and is often in service to an overall vision or to solve a particular need.

This is reflected in the way that Philli designs everything from menus to table settings. In her consultancy, she is given a concept, which she develops from all perspectives, imagining it as an entire functioning system from the customer experience to the payment system, and then seamlessly integrates all these aspects to create a coherent whole.

Multi-sensory understanding and immersion

Philli's exceptional multi-sensory ability is typical of people with dyslexia. Her broad attention to smell, touch, taste, sound and visual design is reminiscent of many designers, artists, chefs and scientists with dyslexia I have spoken to (although the latter are no longer allowed to taste what's in their test tubes as used to be the case!). Again, this can be seen to reflect a more global exploration of the world. Developing multi-sensory understanding comes from learning through experiences. So, it is not surprising that Philli sought to learn through immersion by travelling and working across Japan for nearly a year to experience as many smells, tastes and sights as she could.

TIPS FROM JAMIE

1. Use your imagination

Exploration only comes naturally to some, but anyone can do it. To harness your edge, schedule an annual Exploration Sabbatical and dedicate a week or a month to exploring new opportunities without engaging in exploitation tasks. Afterwards, apply what you've learned to enhance your next project.

2. Think differently

Dyslexic brains are good at seeing the big picture, and it's probably because we explore lots of different areas and spot patterns. I love Philli's idea of displaying flavours as a pie chart. What can you use a pie chart for? Time allocation, resource planning or project spending?

3. Ask, don't guess

No one likes being told what they like, so Philli created a different method of giving customers what they wanted through self-discovery via flow charts. This idea of asking binary questions is a brilliant and fun way to discover what someone wants and needs. To make this work, keep it simple and only use binary (a or b, yes or no) prompts.

CHAPTER 11

NIGEL CABOURN — THE VINTAGE DYSLEXIC

BUSINESS: FOUNDER OF THE ARMY GYM
QUALIFICATIONS: DEGREE

Nigel Cabourn is the designer of iconic utilitarian menswear who gets stopped on the street in Korea and Japan, where he is a household name. He also gets stopped in the UK, but that's usually because of how he's dressed. When we meet, he's wearing an oversized baseball jacket and balloon trousers matched with an outsized baseball cap and several necklaces. He's also sporting two watches, one on each wrist. Let's just say he's not your average looking seventy-something.

Born in Scunthorpe in the north of England in 1949, Nigel later moved to Peterlee, where his dad got a job as a postmaster. He went to the local school, where there were fifty kids in a class and lessons mostly consisted of a teacher writing things on a blackboard. 'I couldn't coordinate somebody talking and writing the stuff down at the same time, so I couldn't take notes. In those days, if you had issues, you were considered a bit stupid.'

And so, like many other people in this book, he was sent to the back of the class and left to figure things out for himself. He didn't even hear the word dyslexia until he was an adult. When he was in his fifties, he mentioned to his mum that he suspected he might be dyslexic. She rejected the idea.

'She went all funny and frowned and said 'Don't talk so bloody stupid.' She was obviously ashamed. I couldn't believe it. I think parents must have taken it as a slur on themselves in the 1950s and 1960s, and she'd carried that feeling on.'

As well as sport, Nigel enjoyed studying history – something that would become a theme in his fashion collections – and his brain for remembering facts and dates was always phenomenal.

'I associate a picture with a date and I know all about the history that really interests me. I know Real Madrid won the European Cup in 1956, '57, '58, '59 and 1960. Or that Michael Hawthorn, the first British guy to win Formula 1, won in 1958. I've got a great memory for when records came out, too.'

He also knows the entire life story of the mountaineer Edmund Hillary. While Nigel has a remarkable skill, it wasn't very helpful when it came to studying academic subjects he wasn't interested in, and he left school with three O levels. Nigel's ambition was to be a footballer like his hero Lev Yashin, the Russian goalkeeper, but when that didn't work out, he looked around for a job. The fashion industry was not on his radar at that point.

'I bumped into a kid who was at technical college with me. He said he'd been to this college in Newcastle and had never seen so many beautiful girls. He said it was a fashion college where you learn how to be a fashion designer. I thought, f*cking hell, that's what I want to do then. So, that's what I did.'

Not only were there several hundred girls at the Newcastle College of Art and Industrial Design, Nigel also realised that he really loved designing clothes.

He also discovered travel. Nigel's mum gave him the bus fare to get from Peterlee to college, but he pocketed the cash and hitchhiked instead. In the summer holidays, Nigel took hitchhiking to the next level and made his way all over Europe without much idea where he was heading. For a man who admits he's never really had a plan for anything, he's travelled – literally and metaphorically – a very long way.

He started to make clothes for fellow students. Though much of what he designed was inspired by the vibrant British music scene in the 1960s, his first label was called Cricket, after the sport.

'At first it was just for pocket money, but then I thought nobody's going to give me a job so I better make it my own business. I was shocked: in 1970 I had a few hundred quid in my pocket, by 1973 I'd bought myself a Porsche and a house.'

Nigel built his business by taking his collections to trade shows around the world. 'I never set anything down on a piece of paper, but I took a few collections to Paris, beautiful collections, and took a stall at shows in Berlin,

Cologne, Paris and New York, and talked to fashion buyers from all over the world.'

He sold his clothes to some of the best department stores on the planet, with a little help from an agent he acquired called Paul Smith. Yes, that Paul Smith. Or, more accurately, Sir Paul Smith, one of Britain's most successful fashion designers of the past century. Paul changed the direction of Nigel's career when he brought him a vintage jacket.

'We were in Paris around 1978, he brought a vintage piece to me, and said, Nige, you should be doing something like this. Look at it, look at the details, this is right up your street. Vintage then became a total reference point for my ideas and I realised that I could buy that piece and that piece, and I put it together like a jigsaw. And that's how I designed.'

Things took off quickly for Nigel after that. The business was rebranded as Nigel Cabourn, and between 1978 and 1980 growth was virtually exponential. 'I went to Paris in 1980 and sold about 30,000 pieces. Sometimes you get lucky and your idea's a hit record. That's what I had in 1980.'

While massive growth is an amazing thing for any business to experience, it can also be destabilising. Almost overnight, Nigel had to ramp up production, and that required an injection of capital. He remortgaged his house, as did his supportive parents. The risk paid off, and for a few years the brand grew and grew. He estimates his turnover was around £3 million in 1980, with an 8 or

10 per cent profit margin. That's about a million in profit in today's money.

Nigel's career – from choosing a college to meet girls, to finding his vintage niche – feels very accidental to me. While he might not have had a map, when he found himself on any particular road, he travelled at lightning speed. 'If you've got energy and enthusiasm, you can do anything really. Talent's probably third, but mostly it's the enthusiasm and the energy to f*cking go out and do it.'

Aside from his talent for design, Nigel's real skill is in finding and collaborating with partners, from paying people to set up the stalls at trade shows to sending his emails. Early on, he hired assistant designers, who worked from his templates.

'I realised that I needed to be the one to sell it, I needed to front it, so I needed people around me to help. I've always had people do everything for me. I don't know whether that's being dyslexic or what, but all the little nitty-gritty stuff, I can't do. I do the creation and the design – that's all coming from me, and I'm pretty clear what I want – but it's important to have people around me that can take my details and make them look attractive.'

Nigel has delegated almost all the functions of running his business. His current PA has been with him twenty-five years and he says that she does everything for him. He dictates emails because he can't use a computer. On the management and compliance side of the business, he is reliant on his chief operating officer (COO). Things move so quickly inside Nigel's head that it is sometimes hard for his team to keep up with him.

'It can be pretty difficult because I lose my temper quite quickly and I'm a bit erratic. But I do my best. I can't read a balance sheet, which is a big problem for me. I just look at the bottom line and make sure it's positive. I'm not very good with figures at all.'

The Nigel Cabourn brand is all about authenticity. His clothes are inspired by military uniforms and workwear from the past, and the materials he uses have to have the same functionality. Where possible, he uses British and European fabrics and many of his items are still made in the UK. When he finds out about a new supplier or manufacturer, he goes to meet them in person. 'I find everyone and everything by word of mouth. I jump in the car at 5 a.m. and drive to Scotland if someone tells me there's a producer I need to know about.'

Nigel's business was transformed by a meeting at the Paris fashion show in the late 1970s when a representative of the Japanese distributor Outer Limits stopped by. In a deal that's lasted over forty years and spawned many shops across Asia, Outer Limits pay Nigel a licensing fee for the Intellectual Property (IP) on his designs, and then manufacture and retail his clothes. I wondered how he felt about giving away ownership of his IP.

'It was all about money coming in, rather than me giving up much. They wanted to take the Nigel Cabourn brand that I was selling in Europe, but not in Japan; they wanted to take part of that and sell it to a network of stores around the Far East. It was a great deal for me. In those days, the only people that had that type of deal would have been Burberry and the big international brands. Outer Limits had just done a deal with Margaret Howell, so she was the first, and that gave me some confidence, and then they did Vivienne Westwood.'

Initially, the deal didn't represent a huge percentage of Nigel's business. He got a few thousand pounds from them for borrowing his name, and in exchange he created some new designs for them. As Outer Limits sold more of Nigel's clothes, the deal expanded. 'Then they bought £300,000 of product off me. These days I've got about a £10 million business in the Far East, with twenty-six stores, and I've still got the same partner today. He's eighty now.'

Nigel currently has four brands. Nigel Cabourn Authentic is still made in England; Nigel Cabourn Mainline is made in Japan; Army Gym is made in Portugal; and his Lybro brand of workwear is produced in Hong Kong.

'I realised that I couldn't survive just making clothes with beautiful rich fabrics made in England. It isn't sustainable. You have to compete with other designers and there comes a stage when you do have to make stuff in Portugal, or China, because of the costs. Getting things manufactured overseas can be a nightmare. It's got lots of pitfalls. You've got to pay for everything using a letter of credit, and to get a letter, you've got to really bankroll it. Generally, if you make a quarter of a million pounds' worth of product from Hong Kong, you've got to find the quarter of a million pounds to fund it. And you've got quality issues. I do a bit of research, which in my case means talking to people as I can't use a computer, and I find the best people. I tend to find anything that's really meaningful to my business comes through word of mouth, and that comes from having good friends in the business.'

Thankfully, Nigel loves the travelling that comes with his job – and he is often away for weeks at a time – saying it's a bit like being a pop star. 'I like everything just so, which means I love to come back to my room and find all my stuff nicely packed, and all clean. It is my character. I stay in great hotels and live like a f*cking lord. And then I meet everybody. I've got a big following because I've got a good smile, I give out good energy, give out good karma. If you give a lot out, you get a lot back. And if you're helpful, people want to help you.'

'Karma' is a word that crops up in Nigel's conversation a lot. 'I really believe in it. I really believe that everything has a reason. I didn't know what karma was when I was younger, but I think I have incredible karma. I am so lucky. Maybe whatever defects I have made me work harder and push myself more. It's all about being positive, happy, giving it out and smiling. It's all connected. That's just how my life has been.'

Nigel's generosity with his time and his energy have helped him build a network that enables his business to thrive, but it became clear when we were talking just how deeply felt his need to give is. He told me a story about giving money to a homeless woman at King's Cross train station when he was stopped by the police because she wasn't allowed to beg on station property. It sounded to me like another illustration of a dyslexic person feeling injustice so deeply that they are moved to change things.

'I very rarely walk past a homeless person. I think you must give out, give out, give out. When the police wouldn't let me give her the fiver in my pocket, she started crying and getting all hysterical. The police moved her on and I felt bad because I hadn't given her the money and she was clearly so desperate. Anyway, I got on my train but I felt terrible. I thought I should get off it and travel back to London, find her and give her the money.'

A lot of Nigel's work is in collaboration with other fashion houses. He's worked with Fred Perry, Vans, Converse and Burberry in recent years. In many ways, these are the perfect arrangements for someone with Nigel's skill set.

'I'm very fortunate that a lot of people come to me who want to collaborate with my brand, and that makes me fairly secure. I design a collection for them, and they do everything else. They use my name, and I get a large sum and give them the designs. I also give them advice on the fabrics. Sometimes I advise them where they should make it. And then I travel to trade shows to represent them, and to be a face.'

When Fred Perry approached him about a collaboration, there was an assumption that the clothing would be themed around tennis (Fred Perry having been a

Wimbledon champion in the 1930s). Nigel had other ideas. In his encyclopaedic brain of sporting facts, he knew that Perry had also been a table tennis world champion in 1929, and so that became the basis for the collection.

'The most important thing is the concept. The way I design generally, I look for a hook, and for Fred Perry it was table tennis. When Diadora approached me, I did a tennis collection for them, and then of course I get obsessed with tennis.'

Even though Nigel is in his mid-seventies, he gets up at 5.30 a.m., six days a week and either plays tennis, table tennis or does strength training with his personal trainer. He openly admits to being obsessive. His all-or-nothing tendency has led him to acquire over 4,000 pieces of vintage clothing that he uses for inspiration. 'I am excessive,' he admits. 'That's why I don't take drugs anymore. If I did, I'd be dead.'

One of Nigel's healthier obsessions has been with Edmund Hillary, the famed mountaineer. He was just a small boy when Hillary became the first person to reach the summit of Everest, and this heroic feat left an impression on Nigel.

'I was saying that I always look for hooks, and hooks for me are often anniversaries. So 2003 was the fiftieth anniversary of Sir Edmund Hillary and Sherpa Tenzing getting to the top of Everest, and I did a collection based on what they were wearing.'

Their achievements had an impact on me too. I was once invited on a four-week trek in Nepal led by Tashi

Tenzing, the grandson of Hillary's partner, who has since become a friend. It is a privilege to get to spend time in the company of someone so closely linked to one of the great milestones in human achievement.

Nigel's obsession meant that when he heard that the jacket Hillary wore on an expedition to the South Pole was on display in a museum in New Zealand, he got on a plane. It's also why he wears two watches, both of which are, naturally, vintage.

'I buy all the books on Hillary for inspiration, and when he went up Everest with the Swiss in 1952 I saw some of the climbers had two watches. And thought, I like the look of that. I did a little bit of research, and when you're climbing mountains, a watch is really important because you need to know your time. If you don't get to the summit in a certain time, you have to come back down before it gets dark, or else you die. So, you have to have two watches in case one packs in.'

Despite his happy-go-lucky demeanour, not everything has worked out for Nigel. Stores in the UK have opened and closed, and he recognises that he lost his way in the early 2000s doing too much consultancy with brands like Berghaus while neglecting his own output.

'But then the fiftieth anniversary of Sir Edmund Hillary's ascent to Everest came up and I just hit lucky. I found those images of Hillary and Tenzing and their clothes were f*cking amazing. I just looked at them and thought, "I'm going to make all those clothes".'

That collection cemented his reputation for a new generation and his brand of authentic outdoor gear is what he's still best known for. Not that it's all plain sailing now. A few months before our interview, he says he was really struggling financially.

'But three months down the line, I've got four jobs on the table. Whenever I'm up against, it just turns. Over the last two or three weeks, I've received half a million pounds' worth of design work, just like that. And that's how it happens for me all the time. Like I say, karma.'

Nigel is one of the very luckiest people in life because he gets to do exactly what he wants to do – indulge in all his passions – and get well paid for it.

'I like buying the vintage, I like to travel, I like to meet people and I like to do what I like doing, which happens to be designing. I'm afraid I don't think I'm a great family man – I love my family, I love my kids, not all my ex-wives – but work-wise I'm not even sure it's strictly work. I just have fun doing my designs. I would say from about 1967, I've just done what I wanted. I'm not even sure I'd call myself a businessman. I'm a designer who owns a business.'

Unsurprisingly, he has no plans to retire. 'Are you crazy? What would I do with myself? No, I'm working till I drop dead. Imagine having nothing to do? No, I'd hate it. *Hate* it.'

INSIGHTS FROM DR HELEN TAYLOR

Recombination

One of the greatest drivers of innovation in the economy is recombination, i.e. taking ideas or information from different sources and combining them in novel ways to make an original creation. We see this in the way that Nigel took different pieces of vintage clothing and put them together to create entirely new designs. People with dyslexia are often exceptional at this because they take inspiration from such a breadth of sources. This isn't completely random, there is often a central theme or need, like vintage in the case of Nigel, a particular customer in the case of Kelly or a restaurant in the case of Philli. But their breadth of experiences provides a broad palette with which to invent.

Complementary Cognition

Delegation is often framed as a coping strategy in people with dyslexia. But as we see illustrated by Nigel, Kelly and others in this book, delegation is what frees them up to do what they are best at. If they were drawn into any one domain of work, they would lose that broad overview which is also critical to creativity.

This is what I have termed 'Complementary Cognition', a new theory that humans have different but complementary ways of learning about the world. In the case of dyslexia, they are specialised to explore broadly in order to understand phenomena at a more global level. This comes at a compromise to achieving narrow, depth-first understanding and detail. I find that, like Cliff and Nigel, dyslexic individuals often collaborate with other people who are good at different procedural or detailed aspects to complement their broader vision. Very often in business that includes a COO, PA or an accountant.

TIPS FROM JAMIE

1. Be the apprentice

It amazes me how many people like the idea of owning a business or being an expert but don't want to wait to learn the ropes. Nigel first made and sold clothes to students at his college, and even Elon Musk worked as a data entry clerk at a bank before becoming the chief executive of PayPal, one of the largest payment businesses in the world.

I recommend people immerse themselves in what they want to do. If you're going to become a CrossFit athlete, would it make sense to train hard while volunteering at your local CrossFit gym or participating in the CrossFit games? Learn the basics of something and see how it informs your perspective.

2. Think global

Dyslexic thinking is big thinking, and dyslexic people often think about global concepts. Nigel quickly visited other countries, leading to his relationship with a

Japanese firm that transformed his business. If he'd not thought globally, Army Gym might not exist. Ask yourself this: would your skills and attributes be more appreciated in a different part of the country or world? If you have yet to find your niche where you live, it could be time to spread your wings.

3. Find a partner

Nigel understands that partnerships are a brilliant way to grow his brand. He's selective about his partnerships, looking for where he can add the most value using his talents and where partners can fill gaps. His dyslexic mind comfortably uses his explorer talent but recognises that execution (exploiter) is not his forte. Many people need help to do this, believing (incorrectly) that you should work on weaknesses rather than simply outsourcing them. What are your talents, where do you need help and who would be your perfect partner?

CHAPTER 12

RICHARD WHITE — THE DYSLEXIC VET

BUSINESS: FOUNDER OF PICKLES
EDUCATION: A LEVELS

I was particularly interested to talk to Richard White because his dyslexia was diagnosed early when he was at school. I wanted to find out if the interventions he had during his education made a difference, and if knowing he was dyslexic had a positive or a negative impact.

His older brother, David, had already been diagnosed with dyslexia and Richard says his parents had their suspicions about him because of his difficulties with reading and writing. Consequently, he was only five or six when he was first tested. He can't really remember the specifics, just the dread and shame of feeling different, of being singled out. With the diagnosis came therapy and interventions.

'My mum was massively into NLP (neurolinguistic programming) back then, so I had NLP and hypnotherapy. There was a specialist who'd developed a programme after, believe it or not, NASA astronauts exhibited dyslexia when they came back to Earth, so the theory was it was to do with imbalance in the inner ear. I was taken to a place in London to do a lot of exercises around balance and juggling to get my neural pathways to work in a different way.'

Richard describes himself as an introverted, quiet kid who didn't like too much attention. 'I didn't mind going somewhere with my mum for tests, but anything at school where I was segregated, I just hated. I didn't want to be different.'

He was given books to read that were for much younger kids that made him feel singled out, and different teachers tried techniques like writing on coloured paper or double-line spacing. Dyslexia was explained to him as his brain working slightly differently.

'I was told you're not good at this or that, and that's what I remember: I wasn't good at things. As a kid, you just want to be normal.' This desire to be normal encouraged him to figure things out for himself.

'I actually felt like I was cheating in maths, but I see now that I was just figuring things out in my own way and I got a lot of gratification from it. That's all I really wanted, to be left alone to figure things out for myself. I wanted the time and space to work through things, but I was always rushed off somewhere else and put through these tests that I didn't understand. To this day, you can't just tell me how something is. I still need to understand how anything works to be able to run with it. The worst-case scenario was a teacher saying, read this in front of the class. It was like having your pants pulled down in front of everyone.'

I got the impression that Richard would have rather not had the interventions his parents and school provided. 'There weren't any stand-out moments where I was called dumb, but it was bit more like, "Oh, Richard, *bless*." It was coming from a good place, but it was a gentle erosion of any kind of self-confidence. The biggest thing with dyslexic people is that we need to instil confidence, self-belief and self-worth. I think the biggest impact of dyslexia is not necessarily the dyslexia itself, but the impact on confidence.'

The upside, as with so many of us, has been resilience. 'I'm a cockroach. You're not going to kill me. If I have a superpower, it's that I can outlast anyone. It's not necessarily a hard thing to do, but I know if I can just hold my nerve and last a little bit longer than the guy next to me, then I'll win.'

Richard went to a very small secondary school with reduced class sizes and an emphasis on building kids' confidence. He was given time, and allowed to do things he was good at, like playing the drums in assembly or DJ'ing at the school disco. With their encouragement, Richard started to apply himself a bit more. He even built his own decks for DJ'ing.

'I loved electronics and taking things apart. It annoyed my dad when I took the laser out of his CD player, but I thought it would be cool to shine a laser on other things. I built a radio to transmit messages and thought about building my own radio mast. I got obsessive about it.'

His favourite shop was Maplins, where he would buy components and build his own electronics. Unfortunately for him, there wasn't a GCSE in tinkering and expectations for his exams were low.

'Writing and thinking at the same time meant I'd miss things. I would just think too fast for what I could write, and my answers fell apart. I was given a scribe for my GCSEs, which was weird. I said my answers out loud and she wrote them down. The first time we did it, it was tough and there was a lot of crossing out and redoing things. The scribe was the headmaster's wife and she gave away lots of telltale signs, so I knew when I'd got something wrong. Then I'd say, no, actually, I think this is what I meant.'

For his second exam, Richard prepared a bit more. 'I went into the room beforehand and I remembered things around the room and attached facts to them. So if there was a noticeboard, I would need to remember this equation or specific fact and attached the data to a physical thing in the room.'

This is something Richard developed for himself, but it is almost identical to a technique I've been taught for public speaking where I'll visit the room beforehand and associate the key points of my speech with specific chairs or pictures or whatever else is in the room. Richard also taught himself magic tricks and this proved helpful in removing awkward social barriers. It's another example of the mechanisms dyslexics develop to cope in a world that isn't built for us.

'The magic wasn't necessarily about impressing people. It was more about not seeming stupid. I can come across as quite socially outgoing, but deep down I'm not. The tricks were a way of giving myself a step up, of getting myself in a safer space socially.'

By the time he was studying for his A levels, Richard had learned how to stand up for himself. 'I was studying business and my teacher returned my essay with red ink all over it. I'd already had a conversation with him and told him that he was not going to solve my spelling problems. He wasn't a nice chap, a bit of a bully, and I remember being physically worked up because I really needed to pass this A level. I went to his office and told him again that it wasn't helpful for him to correct my spelling. I explained that I'd said goodbye to the marks, but what I needed were some notes on the actual content. He just didn't care.'

It amazes, and angers, me that a teacher who *knows* his pupil has dyslexia would do this, but something similar happens to dyslexics every day on social media. I got so bored by the trolls pointing out my spelling mistakes that I gave up on Twitter and Facebook.

As a teenager, it was the activities Richard did outside school that built his confidence, whether that was climbing, magic, DJ'ing – he even set up his own radio station – or being part of the CCF, the Combined Cadet Force.

'I'd made my way up to being the head of the CCF in the army at school, and everyone told me I was good at it. My brother had gone into the army, and I enjoyed the cadets, so it seemed that was the path for me too.

I thought I'd become an officer and get to do a bunch of cool stuff.'

He went to a selection event and was put through his paces on an obstacle course and aced all the physical tests. 'Then they gave us a planning exercise. "You've got a car, you've got this amount of petrol and you've got some casualties over there. You need to come up with an evacuation plan." I just couldn't get my head round it. I started freaking out, thinking, I'm not good at this, I can't do it. And when I had to present my plan, I crumbled. At the very end, they put you on camera to give you your assessment and the guy said, "Don't cry because we'll just laugh at you when we watch the tape back." He told me to go away, get more intelligent and try again in eighteen months. I got the train home, thinking, f*ck, what do I do now? This was my shot and they don't want me.'

These days, Richard has developed tools for situations like that, though he says he still doesn't perform well if he's ambushed. 'I like to think I was capable of working out the problem, but the environment was key. The conditions, the time pressure, it didn't pull the best out of me. These days, I can still go a little bit blank in meetings, and when I start searching for the missing information my memory recall just goes. So I make sure I have triggers in my presentations so that if I draw a blank, I know how to get myself back on track.'

Richard took a year out after his A levels before enrolling at Oxford Brookes University to study for a degree in business. He thought the standard of education was pretty poor, but the nightlife was excellent, and it wasn't long before he dropped out and started organising club nights. He spent everything he earned and eventually realised he wasn't achieving much. He moved to London, where a friend's family ran a pub. He served pints in exchange for rent, but he still wasn't building towards anything. His friend's mum eventually sat him down with the paper open at the job ads: it was time to find a proper job. He got an interview with Foxtons, the estate agent.

'I thought, they're never going to give me a job, but at the interview they make you go round and mingle. I got talking to one of the partners, who asked me what I did in my spare time. I made up some rubbish and said I was a runner. I had picked the one guy in the room who was fanatical about running and racing and I ended up telling him I'd done an Ironman.'

It got him the job. Richard spent the next few years at Foxtons before moving on to another agency. Now in his mid-twenties, he felt he was starting to tread water again. 'I knew I had to figure out what was next. I knew I had some insights into the lettings market, and I saw how frustrating the lettings process could be.'

He developed the idea of a rentals transaction platform that streamlined the entire lettings process, which soon became his first business, Goodlord. As the CEO, Richard's role was to come up with a strategy for the business. It went through a few iterations before finding something that worked. First, they aimed the business at landlords, then at young professionals in house shares, but he found the sweet spot when he pivoted towards medium-sized letting agents.

His co-founder in the business had the connections to bring in funding. 'He came from the start-up world, and we were able to raise £100,000 from angel investors. That was a really proud moment. We'd done a thing that people want to give us money for, and that allowed us to sell it to a few more clients.'

It doesn't take long to burn through that amount of money, and Richard was soon pitching to venture capitalists for the next round of investment. 'We were running out of money, and I was getting to the stage where I just thought this is not going to happen. It had been a good ride, but we were going to have to shut it. But then I got a call out of the blue from a consortium of VCs that wanted to put in £3 million.'

Goodlord made its money from several sources, firstly from selling the platform to the lettings agencies, and then taking fees from everyone who interacted with the platform, whether landlords or tenants. They then sold services, like insurance and surveys, to their customers. As well as leading on the investment side, Richard was also the chief salesperson. 'I knew the lingo, I knew the market, so I was quite good at it.'

Sales and dyslexia seem to go hand in hand, but Richard's dyslexia helped in other ways too. 'The positives are that I'm quite a good thinker, and that's separate from problem solving. I think things through in a way that seems logical to me, and I think my logic allows me to take more risks and go after things that other people wouldn't. The downsides are that I sometimes struggle to communicate what I want to my team. I find I sometimes need to say something eight different times, in eight different ways. There are some high-pressure situations where, if I don't feel confident, there are triggers that put me back in a certain space. If I'm not feeling confident in a situation, then the outcome is not going to be good. It's a psychological hump I have that if I'm in the wrong frame of mind, I can't communicate.'

Clearly, Richard did handle the big pressure moments because Goodlord raised £13 million for its Series A round of funding, receiving backing from some very well-respected venture capital firms. But it was just at this moment that his relationship with his co-founder started to break down and he left the company.

With his partner gone, Richard single-handedly oversaw the rapid expansion from thirty staff to a team of 130, including thirty or forty developers who redesigned the platform ahead of an industry-wide rollout.

'But that inflection point never came. We never delivered the tech and it became awkward with the investors. We had a few million left in the bank at this stage and I levelled with them, saying that I had been too trusting with the developers and had overtrusted their timeframes. I lost the credibility with them to say, this is the plan, this is how we will move forward.'

Richard is involved with YPO, the Young Presidents Organisation, which offers support and networking for young entrepreneurs. He knows from other members of YPO that the pressure he was under from his investors wasn't unique.

'It's a crazy scenario to give a twenty-something a bunch of millions without putting the right structures in place. There are a lot of people who get put in impossible situations with no support. I know now that they weren't even investing their own money, and they would have questions to answer if they didn't invest their allocation. When you're in that world you see how similar everyone is, down to the clothes they wear and the language they use. They're looking for people who are similar to them to invest in and they found me. I think that's because if things go wrong, there isn't someone on their board saying I told you that person was a wild card. With me, they could say we were just unlucky this time.'

People will always look for someone to blame when a start-up doesn't deliver, and as CEO, Richard would have been in the firing line whether or not he had put his hands up. Like many other interviewees in this book, Richard wasn't afraid of making mistakes or owning up to them, so he put his hands up and accepted some of the blame. His investors were happy to tell their boards that they had found their fall guy. Richard was given a severance package and asked to leave the company he'd founded. Only his cockroach-like resilience would get him through the years ahead.

'I was incredibly sad to go. I didn't want to let it go, it was part of my identity. But if I'm honest, there was also absolute relief that it wasn't my problem anymore. Running these things is emotionally hard and it takes it out of you. It probably took eighteen months to stop the negative emotions. I wouldn't say I was bullied, but I was manipulated. One of the investors later told me that I was very 'easy' and that I hadn't made it an issue for them.'

Richard was supported, financially and emotionally, by his partner Hayley, who brings in a reliable salary as a corporate lawyer. This afforded him some time to develop what he would do next. He was actively looking for a market, a bit like the lettings arena, where technology could simplify transactions and boost bottom lines. His research led him towards veterinarian practices.

After his exit from Goodlord, Richard was eager to prove himself. 'There were a few false starts of thinking "this is the thing, this is my angle". It was two years of putting together a network by just turning up at dog groomers with doughnuts and having a conversations. If I wanted to get to the next step, I had to know the industry, I had to be credible, and that takes a long time.'

He formalised his research by setting up Pet-Tech, a networking service for anyone in the pet industry. He put on events that every attendee benefitted from, but no one got as much out the sessions as Richard.

'It was a vehicle where I could speak to the right people at the big companies and get the lie of the land. Otherwise you're just reading the trade press and not getting the full picture. You have to talk to hundreds of people to figure out what's happening and map out the trends in an industry. What are the weak spots? Where are the pressure points? In some cases it was that the companies were more interested in making their shareholders happy than their customers. There had also been an unbundling of services in the sector, which meant people weren't taking their pets as frequently to the vets as they should do.'

Initially, Richard leaned towards replicating what Goodlord had done for lettings agencies. 'I realised that rinse and repeat was not going to work. All my market research showed that building the software and the systems wasn't enough; we actually needed to operate the vets' practices too.'

Pickles, named after a beloved pet dog that died, is still in the early stages. They opened their first branch in west London in 2023 and have plans to open fifteen branches within two years. The branding has more in common with a desk-sharing office in Brooklyn or Clerkenwell, and it intentionally feels like a club because it is one. Instead of pet owners paying per visit, they pay an annual membership fee of £120 and can see a vet as often as they need. Operations and prescriptions are extra.

'Rather than taking a short-term view of trying to extract as much value out of the pet owner in the shortest space of time, we have a lifetime relationship with the pet and offer a greater amount of value to the owner.'

Richard has raised finance from investors to get him to this stage, and once the concept is proven he'll look to bring in venture capital investment to roll out Pickles further. Despite now running his second venture, Richard shies away from the label 'entrepreneur'.

'I don't know where it comes from, but I've always had a weird aversion to the word. I'd never introduce myself as an entrepreneur. If someone asks me what I do, I simply say I run a business.'

I'm also reluctant to overuse the label, and I wonder if in Richard's case it's more about a rejection of labels entirely. When you've been singled out in school for being different, I can understand the instinct to recoil from labelling yourself in adulthood. I wanted to know how Richard's dyslexia was still impacting his work life.

'As long as no one is asking me to read a document out loud, or give them a breakdown of its contents in twenty minutes, I'm fine. In my own time, and if there's a reason for me to read something, I'm actually quite good at reading it through and working out the mechanics of things. But if I have no vested interest, then I don't bother.'

When it comes to preparing documents, there are now tools available to him that didn't exist when he was at school. 'Some people still think I should use Grammarly for every email, but if they understand what I mean, I think it's their problem not mine. It's different for investor reports or important documents. I've used ChatGPT to improve something I've written. It's an iterative process; you can't just chuck something in and expect it to write something flawless. I also occasionally create a Google Doc and share that with a couple of trusted people to review before sending it out.'

Talking to Richard, I spotted a recurring theme in his life that is linked to his dyslexia: injustice. Whether it was an A-level business teacher's red ink all over his homework, or the VCs who sacked him from Goodlord, it was clear to me that Richard is driven by unfairness and righting wrongs.

'Injustice runs through my life. If I feel an injustice is being done to anyone or anything, that's what motivates me. There is a sense of fairness that I believe in so strongly, and sometimes that's difficult because life isn't always fair. It's where a lot of my emotion comes from. If I feel I've been slighted, then that lights a fire in me.'

Far from being a disadvantage, Richard says dyslexia is what gives him his edge. 'All my businesses are problem-solving businesses. My special power is seeing the world for what it is, seeing the problem, soaking up all the information, ingesting it, and seeing if there's a business to be made out of that problem. As much as dyslexia brings negatives, it also gives me an edge over most things and most people.'

INSIGHTS FROM DR HELEN TAYLOR

Communication difficulties

As we've seen throughout this book, people with dyslexia seem to build up a more global, complex, interconnected understanding of the world. This may lie at the heart of the many talents they possess, but as we see with Richard, it can also make communication difficult. For one, it can be hard to know where to start, because in a network there is no obvious beginning point or linear structure. It can also be difficult if the audience doesn't already have some familiarity with aspects of what is to be explained. Connections that might be obvious to the individual with dyslexia are often not obvious to other people. Also, when there are many interconnections, with thoughts often being non-verbal and visual, it can be difficult to translate these ideas clearly into words so another person can understand them.

Communication strengths

As for everyone, anxiety and stress can compound communication difficulties, but when relaxed, people with dyslexia can become 'endowed with the gift of silver tongues' as MacDonald Critchley, a world-renowned professor in dyslexia research, put it. Very often, people with dyslexia are natural storytellers, which isn't surprising when you consider that telling a story is an ideal way to communicate relationships and connections. They can also be enthusiastic and persuasive speakers, as reflected in everything from their talent in sales and a 'gift of the gab' to the ability to motivate and unite, as seen in the speeches of notable dyslexics Lloyd George or Winston Churchill.

TIPS FROM JAMIE

1. Invent something

Dyslexics often innovate naturally as we see solutions to problems that others can't. This led to Thomas Edison inventing the light bulb, Alexander Graham Bell the telephone and the Wright brothers achieving the first powered flight. Richard saw a problem with renters, and the administration required to take on a lease, so he created the tech platform Goodlord (what a great name, by the way). What problems can you see, and which can you solve by investing in something new?

2. Maintain deep focus

Dyslexic thinkers can concentrate intensely on subjects that interest them. Richard demonstrates this with his obsessive market research. Try this yourself: the next time you need to complete a task, drop everything else, remove all distractions (phones, TVs and music players) and lock yourself in a room, promising only to leave once you have completed the task.

3. Use your sense of injustice

Think of a time when something made you angry and try to work out why. Harness that anger and use it as motivation to find solutions. You might develop a whole new way of helping customers that will impress your boss or enhance your bottom line.

CHAPTER 13

KATE GRIGGS – THE DYSLEXIC SOCIAL ENTREPRENEUR

BUSINESS: FOUNDER OF MADE BY DYSLEXIA
QUALIFICATIONS: O LEVELS

Kate Griggs is the founder of a charity called Made By Dyslexia that campaigns to change how dyslexia is understood and how dyslexic kids are taught in schools. Kate and her team have achieved an incredible impact and to date, Made By Dyslexia's training has been taken by over a million teachers worldwide, impacting the education – and life chances – of tens of millions of children across the globe.

In many ways, Kate's entire life has been shaped by dyslexia. Even though her older brother Tom had been diagnosed as dyslexic, Kate struggled in silence, echoing Chef Philli's experience of coping without support, despite her brother's dyslexia being recognised. 'Like a lot of girls, I just kept my head down and tried to work hard, but I was failing miserably and feeling really stupid because I couldn't do the work the other kids could do.'

To help Tom, her parents paid for the Orton-Gillingham method that uses multisensory phonics to teach reading. Kate absorbed some of Tom's lessons and when she started school, her reading wasn't too bad.

'But my comprehension was terrible, my maths was terrible, my sequential memory was terrible. I didn't know my times tables. Like a typical dyslexic, when the round-robin reading was happening, I'd be sitting there waiting for my turn, knowing that I'd be able to read it but I'd be stumbling over my words.'

Nevertheless, her dyslexia wasn't picked up. Like a lot of kids, Kate loved animals and wanted to be a vet when she grew up. She knew she'd need to be good at biology to become one, and thankfully she really enjoyed those classes. 'My biology teacher was also my maths teacher, and I hated maths, I was terrible at it, and when I said I wanted to be a vet, she said, "Oh, you're not clever enough to do that".' What a crushing thing to say to an enthusiastic child.

When Kate was approaching the age to take the Common Entrance exam – a test taken by kids hoping to go to a private secondary school in the UK – the headmistress called her parents in to school.

'She basically said that I wasn't very bright. I was a very nice girl who tried hard and I had quite a pretty face so could probably marry well, which back in the 1960s was the sort of thing people would say. My father was not having this, and literally the following week I was removed from the school and taken to Millfield Prep.

I relayed to the headmaster all the things that I'd been told – that I wasn't very bright, wasn't going to be able to pass exams and probably wouldn't be able to do much in life – and he said, "It sounds like you're probably dyslexic. We can give you all the help you need to do as well as you can in exams, but we don't really care about exams. What matters is what you're good at and what you're passionate about, and what makes you come to school to learn." He said, "It's those things, those thinking skills, that will make you successful in life".'

It was a life-changing moment, and Kate was just one of many whose lives were changed by Millfield Prep. Set up in the 1930s in Somerset, south-west England, Millfield has always taken a different approach to education and values success in non-academic areas as highly as exam results.

'I'm not super artistic or musical or mega creative like my brother, who was really good at art and making things with his hands. But the thing they recognised in me was leadership and they piled responsibility on me really early. They could see that I had good people skills and good leadership skills. I probably would never have thought I had leadership skills because the experience at my first school had made me really shy. I just did not want anybody to notice who I was, because going under the radar was a lot less painful. What was lovely was that Millfield could see that I had those natural leadership skills. I hated bullying, so there would always be people who I would take under my wing, and they were very good at recognising that, which was amazing.'

They also recognised her love of animals and put her in charge of them in the science labs. Kate showed some early entrepreneurial flair when, as head lab monitor, she realised how quickly guinea pigs breed.

'I bought a pedigree male and a female long-haired Abyssinian guinea pig – they weren't expensive at all and looked like Dougal from *The Magic Roundabout* – and let them breed. Then I sold the babies to all my friends and put ads in local newspapers.'

With the encouragement and support of Millfield teachers, Kate passed a handful of O levels and stayed on to study for A levels. But midway through her course, her father's business took a downturn and the family could no longer afford the fees.

'The late 1970s was not a great time in the UK. There were haulage strikes and my dad's was a peat company – he invented grow bags for vegetables – that used postal and haulage services. His business had worked well for an awfully long time, but the whole of Britain was in a terrible mess. It was not that his business was badly run, it was that really bad things were happening. I felt very sad for my dad, and I would have liked to have finished my education, but change happens. You move on.'

Kate was considering a career in marketing or journalism and, aged sixteen, moved to London. She stayed with friends for a while, seeking a job in the hotel industry where accommodation was included. She later found employment in advertising, where she worked for a couple of different agencies before moving on to work for a music publisher. When she had her first child, Ted, in 1993, Kate went freelance. It wouldn't be until Ted started school that she discovered what her mission in life would be.

'I could tell that Ted was dyslexic from about three years old. I was dyslexic myself, as was my whole family, so I knew what to look for. Ted would be an absolute expert in certain things. He would know the name of every single dinosaur. He could tell you whether they were a herbivore or a carnivore. He would draw them – and they were absolutely brilliant drawings – but he could barely write his name and he had absolutely no interest in reading books. He loved being told stories, though. Loved TV. Loved anything to do with nature. He was also very musical and loved dancing and singing. He had these clear, obvious talents and passions, but with his schoolwork, there was just no interest whatsoever. He really didn't want to knuckle down to anything and, for me, he was clearly a kid that wasn't ready to be in a pushy academic school environment. He just needed to be left to be creative.'

Kate assumed that in the decades since she had left school, the education system would have learned lessons from schools like Millfield and found a way to teach children with divergent abilities.

'I told his school I was pretty sure he was dyslexic and they looked at me slightly strangely when I asked if they could just keep an eye out for it. At that time, kids would come home with these little boxes full of words that you had to put together. Ted would look at them and he had no idea what anything was. He got very frustrated with it and used to throw it around, saying, "I can't do this, Mummy." I kept going into school and saying I'm sure he's dyslexic. They kept saying no, he's a boy, he's late developing. You don't need to worry about it.'

But Kate was worried. Whenever she was in the school, she couldn't help but notice that Ted never had any of his work on the wall, which must have made him feel terrible.

'We noticed that he started getting less confident. More anxious. Then one day, when he was five years old, I was reading him his bedtime story, and he said, "Mummy, what do I need to do to not wake up in the morning?" I said what do you mean, and he said, "Well, if I don't wake up, I haven't got to go to school." That was heartbreaking to hear.'

Kate had tears in her eyes as she recalled this moment, as did I, and I would like everyone reading this – especially if you work in education or government and can influence how dyslexia is perceived – to reflect on this. A five-year-old boy found school so miserable that he didn't want to wake up. This is why it is so important that we change the narrative around dyslexia. 'Then everything poured out. Ted said that the other children had told him there was something wrong with his brain because he couldn't do the work they could do. The teacher shouted at him.'

Kate insisted again that Ted was tested for dyslexia – this time at her expense – and the results showed, as she had long suspected, that he was. Kate was so angry that her suspicions about dyslexia had been dismissed, and Ted had been made to feel so bad, that she knew she had to do something about it.

'This was supposed to be a very, very good school,' she says. 'They should've known better and they told me they did know better, but it transpired that none of the teachers had any training in dyslexia, which I was shocked about.' Clearly, paying fees is no guarantee of getting a good education when you're dyslexic.

The staff at Millfield School had known how to teach dyslexic kids in the 1930s. Kate had experienced how transformational this could be in the 1970s: it seemed unfathomable to her that as the UK approached the end of the 20th century, the educational establishment hadn't learned the same lessons.

Initially motivated to help Ted, Kate enrolled on a course in how to teach learners with dyslexia, at the Helen Arkell Dyslexia Centre in Farnham, Surrey. She had kicked up such a stink at Ted's school that one of his teachers was also on the course.

On the course, Kate learned how hit-and-miss it is whether or not teachers have any training in dyslexia, or even know the skills and strengths associated with it. 'What I learned is that in mainstream education, we are measuring and treasuring the wrong things.'

Kate realised that if she carried on with the training, she could have an impact on Ted's education, but if she could change the way teachers approach dyslexia more generally, she could have an impact on hundreds of thousands, if not millions, of children's education. She and her husband made the decision to send Ted and his younger brother Will, who Kate was also confident was showing indicators of dyslexia, to Millfield.

'When I started doing the training I realised that so many parents were in the same position as me. Once I understood how bad things were in both the private and state education systems, I thought I had to change things. It just wasn't right that it had been going on for decades.'

Like any other entrepreneur who sees something that can be changed, Kate spotted an opportunity.

'I think if you talk to most dyslexic entrepreneurs, when they see something that could be better, they want to make that change. It's what motivates them. It's not usually the money that motivates them. Richard Branson wanted to make airlines better. For me, it was as clear as anything: the difference between dyslexic children in Britain succeeding and failing was whether or not the teachers were trained. Kids leaving school unable to read and write is a huge disgrace, and a lot of them are unsupported dyslexics. A lot of the kids with behavioural problems who end up being excluded from school are also often unsupported dyslexics. And then if you look at substance abuse, alcohol abuse, depression, prisons, all of those things, they have an over-representation of dyslexic people who've not been supported. Ted was growing up in a loving, supportive, dyslexia-friendly home, and he was being made to feel like he didn't want to wake up. Imagine adding poverty and disadvantage and not understanding dyslexia into that equation?'

Kate's dyslexic brain had identified a problem – the poor understanding of dyslexia in education – and had found a solution: training teachers. Under the wing of the Helen Arkell Centre, Kate set up an organisation called Xtraordinary People in 2005. Initially, it was just her and its aim was to change the way dyslexic kids were taught in schools.

'In order to train teachers, I knew we needed support from government. All the teacher training in the UK was provided by either the Helen Arkell Centre, the British Dyslexia Association or Dyslexia Action, all of which are charities and none of them were having conversations with government. Unless there was a united voice, it was going to be very difficult for me, as a completely unknown person, to create change.'

Successive governments had failed to change the status quo, and Kate realised this was because they thought it was too big a problem to solve. 'If you lump all special education needs together, it probably is too big a problem to solve, unless you have millions and millions of pounds. But if you separate it out, and you look at dyslexia on its own, it's such a simple fix. We need every teacher trained in how to create an inclusive classroom that supports dyslexic children, and then we need some teachers who can give the extra support to the kids in need.'

Apart from the Helen Arkell Centre, Kate had no contacts at any of the other dyslexia charities, but she did know Sir Richard Branson, the founder of all things Virgin, through her brother, who had been instrumental in setting up Virgin Mobile. Once she had Richard on board, she made contact with the TV chef Jamie Oliver, and then the singer Robbie Williams. She wanted to make sure dyslexia had a loud voice, and the best way to create noise is by having celebrities supporting you.

Despite the celebrity endorsements, Kate found it hard to make headway with the Department for Education. She decided she needed to create some sort of stunt that got her on the radar of government. Ruth Kelly, the education secretary at the time, was in a precarious parliamentary seat. Kate came up with the idea of forming the Xtraordinary People Political Party and standing against Kelly at the next general election.

Not long after Kate's name was included on the official list of candidates, she had a call from one of Ruth Kelly's special advisers. Concerned that she might take votes away from Kelly, they wondered if Kate would stand aside if the secretary of state supported her aims. 'I said, of course, and I had a meeting with Ruth, who said that if she was elected, we would sit down and have further meetings.'

Job done, or so Kate thought. But after Ruth Kelly was re-elected, Kate didn't get her promised appointment at the Department for Education. 'All the phone numbers had changed. And I tried writing to her, and just got completely blanked.'

Undeterred, Kate went to the media with her story and was invited on *Good Morning Britain*, one of the UK's most watched breakfast TV shows, where she got to confront Ruth Kelly on her broken promise live on TV.

'She wasn't in the studio, she was in her office in Westminster, and she said they understood that they needed to learn more and were talking to the British Dyslexia Association. I was able to say that I knew they weren't, because we were working with the British Dyslexia Association. As soon as I came out of the studio, I had a call from the minister for schools.'

Despite creating waves, it was becoming obvious that nothing was going to change quickly enough for Kate, or for the kids at school who needed the kind of help Ted was now getting at Millfield.

Kate kept up the pressure on government by working with a documentary team at the BBC. *Teacher Squad* took the worst-performing Year 7 pupils (aged eleven) at a secondary school in inner London and gave them teachers who were trained in multi-sensory education, which gives kids a chance to learn through talking, moving, touching and listening rather than just reading and writing.

'Sixty-five per cent of kids leaving primary school unable to read, write or add up are unidentified or unsupported dyslexics. We took those kids that nobody else wanted, the naughty kids, the kids who'd left primary school unable to read and write, and we screened them all for dyslexia and put in the support they needed. We saw these kids transform in front of our eyes, and in just two terms, children went from being really naughty to suddenly learning. Diagnosis is such a turning point for any dyslexic person, because suddenly you've got a reason for all the things that you're ashamed of. So many dyslexic people think they're not good enough, but dyslexia also explains these incredible talents you've got. If you're a government that wants to make sure every child can read, you have to address how we teach dyslexics.'

Ministers from the Department for Education visited the school and that led to the government investing £10 million in teacher training. Although that represented substantial investment, it was never going to be enough to transform the opportunities for every child who needed the system to change.

Kate was on her way to becoming a leading voice in dyslexia. She might not have a doctorate or letters after her name, but her campaigning work had helped her develop significant insights into the systemic challenges, as well as some of the potential solutions. To create the change she knew was needed, and was possible, Kate could not wait for things to move at the speed of the Department for Education. Besides, the UK wasn't the only country that would benefit from incorporating dyslexia awareness into its teacher training.

Kate set up Made By Dyslexia, an organisation with the ambition to provide free training for every school and workplace in the world to empower dyslexic thinking. 'I think when you find your purpose in life, you just make these massive leaps, and our mission as a charity is not to exist. If we're going to achieve that, then we have to move really, really fast.' By 2030, she wants to have transformed the way dyslexia is understood so comprehensively that the services offered by Made By Dyslexia will no longer be needed.

Knowing that you can't achieve much on your own, Kate teamed up with organisations like Ernst & Young and secured endorsements from famous dyslexics, including Princess Beatrice. Made By Dyslexia has simultaneously changed perceptions about dyslexia and is transforming the way institutions cater for, and harness, dyslexic thinking. Thanks to their partnerships, Made By Dyslexia has created hours of online training that any teacher, or any business, can access for free. 'We've worked with world-leading dyslexia schools to plan our lessons and we've worked with Microsoft, who can make sure those lessons are in every single language and are free and accessible on their platform.'

Rather than changing the world one teacher at a time, Made By Dyslexia is turbo-charging change by working with major institutions.

'Our mission is to train every single teacher. In order to do that, we are going to have to have some really big wins. I'd read that the mayor of New York, Eric Adams, was dyslexic. So, I thought, if I can get the biggest city in the world to use our training, then that's a big statement. I reached out to all the people I know in the dyslexia world and said I wanted to meet the mayor of New York.'

A few phone calls later, Kate was speaking to the mayor's chief of staff. By securing New York City, Kate was making a big enough statement that other cities would want to follow. Millions of teachers have now taken Made By Dyslexia's courses. *Millions.* And they are transforming education and life outcomes for tens of millions of kids.

But for Kate, that's not enough. Made By Dyslexia is also working to change attitudes to dyslexia in the workplace with more free online courses for HR departments and employers. With this programme, Kate won't just be improving things for dyslexic employees, she'll be improving these companies' bottom lines as they learn to harness the benefits of dyslexic thinking. NYC has already committed to getting all their staff to participate in Kate's workplace training. She has also reached out to Gavin Newsom, the governor of California, to do the same on the West Coast. Additionally, Kate has teamed up with LinkedIn Learning, who rarely offer anything for free, to offer workplace training. She says having Richard Branson involved was key as they could see it was a course that was going to be picked up by everybody.

Kate's greatest skill is undoubtedly networking. 'My husband always says I'm the most amazing connector, not in the way of having lots of friends, but just knowing how to reach the right people. Honestly, you just have to ask. I was three degrees of separation from the mayor of New York's chief of staff. I was two degrees away from Gavin Newsom's chief of staff.'

As we came to the end of our conversation, I was starting to think that there is nothing Kate couldn't achieve if she put her mind to it, and this is because she has such a deep sense of purpose.

'If I fail, I fail. And I'm not scared of failing. I think it's just something that happens. If it's meant to be, it'll happen, you just have to push and push and push. And when things don't happen, there's normally something much better around the corner. Failure doesn't worry me. If I fail, then I'll find another way around, but when some people fail they just never pick themselves up. Everybody needs to learn how to fail.'

Crucially, Kate's story shows that entrepreneurial talents aren't only used to make money. Dyslexic skills are change-making skills. Transformative skills. No matter what organisation you are in, whether it's a Fortune 500 business or a non-government organisation, you should find as many people who think the way Kate does, and work as hard as she does, to create the change you want to see in the world.

INSIGHTS FROM DR HELEN TAYLOR

Multi-sensory learning

The success of teachers trained in multi-sensory education – using talking, moving, touching and listening rather than just reading and writing – can be understood in the context of the other stories we've heard in this book. From Kelly, who talked about the importance of smell, touch and sound as well as visual senses in designing, to Theo, who described how he could sense and feel things in social situations, and Philli, who even considered the sounds of the food she made, experiencing the world in a highly multi-sensory way is often typical of people with dyslexia. It therefore makes sense that a more multi-sensory or, as we've seen, immersion approach to learning can be beneficial.

Indeed, for most of human existence, we would have learned through 'apprenticeship' learning. Modern European education systems mostly have their origins in religious institutions that were primarily for training the clergy, with a focus on literacy and religious texts. This shaped the nature of education, which has remained primarily text-based, in contrast to the more hands-on learning approach that existed for the majority of human existence.

Social networking

Kate is clearly exceptional at social networking: from connecting with business people like Richard Branson to celebrities and royalty, she's succeeded in building a network to support her in reaching her goals. This exceptional social networking ability is often seen in people with dyslexia. Again this can be viewed through the lens of exploration, but exploring in social rather than physical space.

Just as with concepts and ideas, people with dyslexia often make unusual social connections. They might connect someone they just met with a person they knew ten years ago, realising that they are puzzle pieces that together solve a problem, or that one could help another get their dream job.

TIPS FROM JAMIE

1. Stories are better with emotion

Kate's story is so heartfelt that it's impossible not to want to listen to, understand and support her cause. Can you imagine hearing your child say, 'What can I do to not wake up in the morning?' Heartbreaking. It brings tears to my eyes just writing these words.

What's your story? And what's the emotional hook to make people remember you? Take time to think about this and remember that humans often recall the bad more often than the good. Content that triggers adverse emotional reactions such as anger, fear or sadness are also more likely to be shared. But a warning: your stories must be genuine, authentic and relevant.

2. Take the shortcut

We heard earlier that dyslexic thinkers often want to get from A to Z but miss out on the B to Y, and Kate is no different. Kate wanted every teacher in the world to learn how to identify dyslexia. Rather than develop a strategy of communicating with every school and government globally, she found the biggest and the best platform to reach these people in one go: LinkedIn, one of the world's most powerful education brands. With a mission as big as Kate's – to train every school and workplace in the world to empower dyslexic thinking with free training – it's easy to see why LinkedIn would be the perfect partner. It has almost one billion users in over 200 countries.

What shortcut can you create to get the outcome you desire?

3. Use your network

Like me, Kate wanted to make a difference to those impacted by dyslexia. Kate thought strategically, so she used her contacts to get to arguably the most famous dyslexic entrepreneur on the planet, Sir Richard Branson, to support her cause. This allowed her to launch with a bang and use the Branson brand to rally other support.

The six degrees of separation theory suggests everyone is connected by, at most, six interpersonal links. Kate realised this and used her network to continue to get influencers. Consider this: she was only three steps away from the mayor of New York and two connections from the governor of California's chief of staff. But that was only because she made her first connection.

Who do you need to connect with? How can you use a platform such as LinkedIn to make those connections? Please don't overthink this; several of the contributors in this book came after I made an initial connection this way. You have nothing to lose and everything to gain from expanding your network.

CHAPTER 14

JAMIE WALLER — THE DYSLEXIC ENTREPRENEUR

BUSINESS: FOUNDER OF LOVE YELLOW
QUALIFICATIONS: NONE

I asked my wife if I should include my own story in this book and she suggested that if I didn't, I'd regret not sharing something that might help others. Whereas if I did, someone reading this might think if he could achieve so much, then maybe so can I. So here goes.

Like many in this book, I was told I would never amount to anything. But by the time I was twenty-two, I had started three businesses and by the time I was thirty, I'd made a few million pounds and was something of a TV star.

I grew up in Bethnal Green, in the East End of London, in the 1980s, where I lived with my parents in a flat above a shop. We had very little. My mum was employed as a carer and my dad worked in demolition. Like a lot of families on our street, we lived from payday to payday.

When my mum passed away in 2014, I found my old school reports and it was a surprise to read that, in primary school at least, I wasn't considered stupid. I got all As, Bs and Cs. But when I reached age nine and ten, and they expected more from me academically, it was noticeable that the comments were all about effort, rather than my attainment.

I loved primary school, and my friends were bright kids who all passed the test to get into Raine's Foundation, the best secondary school in the area. I didn't make the grade and was sent to a rough all boys' school at the end of my street. It felt like I'd lost my friends overnight.

Nevertheless, on my first day of secondary school, I put on my uniform and shined my shoes. I'd learned how to tie a tie at the right length, so it sat just above my belt buckle, and walked in with my little bag, ready to learn. I honestly thought it was going to be great. I have a vivid memory of entering the playground and seeing all these scruffy kids in ties tied so small that you could just about see the bottom part of the triangle. Most didn't even have blazers. They were definitely more street smart than me and they spotted the innocence written all over my face. The bullying started in that first break time.

The bullying led to me bunking off, and soon the teachers assumed I didn't want to learn. They sent me to the back of the class, where I listened to music on my headphones. Before long, I was so far behind I knew I would never catch up.

When I eventually stood up to my bully, I hit him over the head with a chair. I was immediately suspended and eventually expelled. Things were even worse at my new school, and when my mum was diagnosed with breast cancer when I was fourteen, I stopped going all together.

It was only thanks to the founders of a charity I had been supported by since I was five – a motorcycle display team called the Imps – that I was given another chance at Raine's Foundation, the school I'd always wanted to go to. The headmaster let me join on the condition that I agreed to show up. That's all, just show up. I later found out his own mother was suffering with breast cancer, and that was why he was willing to help. Armed with that information, I knew I could not let Mr Lewis down.

It worked, and I did well enough to be invited to sit a handful of GCSEs, the first of which was history. It was also my last. The Portakabin where the test took place was filled with folding wooden desks that were covered in graffiti tags from previous exam sitters. Every kid wrote their name and the date of the exam on them. It was like a ritual. I'd even brought a marker pen with me especially. I got out my marker and wrote Waller, then a big line underneath, and then the date. And as I did it, the teacher walked up to me and asked to see me outside. Because I had been using a pen before the official exam started, they were disqualifying me. End of discussion. I walked back through the school yard, and I just cried.

I wandered through several different housing estates, sobbing the whole time. When I eventually got home, my mum gave me a hug, but I couldn't stop crying. I told her that I couldn't go back. She said if I found a job before my next exam, then I didn't have to sit it. That afternoon I went out and got myself a job as a labourer on a building site earning £35 a day for carrying bricks.

My experience of school had an enormous impact on my confidence. If there's an upside, it's that when you change schools that many times, you learn to be resilient and a good networker. Bethnal Green was rough. People weren't just getting beaten up, they were getting stabbed, so not fitting in had consequences. You were forced to make new friends and to find ways to make them like you, and that turned out to be a crucial, life-changing skill.

My first business was a window cleaning round. I paid a local window cleaner to show me how to do it, then went and got myself clients by knocking on doors and utilising my ability to make people like and trust me. While cleaning the windows of a newsagent's on Woolwich Road, I noticed there was a vacant plot next door. There were second-hand car dealers all along that stretch of road, and I wondered why no one had done the same on that vacant spot. I asked the newsagent if I could rent the yard (if I promised to still clean his windows) and suddenly I had my second business.

Looking back, I was so naïve. Thanks to the Imps Motorcycle Display Team, I knew my way around an engine, and I found out there was a formula to valuing second-hand cars that is laid out in the industry bible, *Parkers*. Buying and selling cars was the easy bit. Paying business rates? I'd never heard of them. Planning permission? Who knew you needed permission to change the use of a piece of land? Certainly not eighteen-year-old me. The rates I duly paid, but I got around the planning issue by parking the cars on the street. They were the only ones that had the price boards in the windscreens. If anyone official asked, the cars in the yard were 'customer parking' for the newsagent next door. But if a customer showed an interest in the cars on the street, then I showed them the 'parked' ones too. The fines for parking on the single yellow line that ran all the way along that stretch simply became a cost of doing business. I was making a profit of £1,000 a week. Not bad for a teenager in the late 1990s.

The dyslexic brain is always looking for workarounds because that's what it's good at. If you can't do things the conventional way, you figure out a different way to do things, and I was always looking for more ways to make money. Could I hire out the cars? Could I start a taxi business? I was actively looking for opportunities to make myself a millionaire. I really wanted to be rich.

With the rates bill and the parking fines and the planning issues, I was starting to feel hard done by. I felt that I was a young man trying to do the right thing and society was out to get me. Then, one day, Woolwich Road was closed and I didn't know why. I soon found out though: Transport for London was painting double red lines all along the street that would run right past my yard. A double red line doesn't just mean no parking, it means no stopping, and the penalties for infringement were punishing. Not only could I no longer park my cars on the street, but my customers wouldn't be able to pull over and take a look. It was the end of my business, and I knew it.

I'm sure there must have been a consultation period, but I was young and naive and I didn't get that memo. There was nothing I could do about it. It felt personal. They were taking my business away from me. *They* were doing it to *me*. I felt victimised. I know now that it wasn't personal, but as a teenager my sense of injustice veered towards rage.

I watched a local TV news report about the new red lines that featured market traders saying they would refuse to pay any fines. Then a man from Transport for London came on and said they would collect the fines from non-payers through enforcement agencies. I just thought, 'Bloody hell, there we go, *that* is going to be huge.' I knew I'd found my idea for my next business.

I talked my way into a job with a debt collection agency and quickly found out that the work wasn't all that different from selling cars. Like so many businesses, collecting debts was about sales, which is basically about removing the barriers to people saying yes. Even back then, I considered myself to be a good salesperson. My gift of the gab was the reason I did well initially, but the reason I didn't throw in the towel after six months of working in a very difficult industry was due to the sense of injustice I felt. When I saw that some of my colleagues were simply terrorising people for money, I thought there had to be a better way.

As a kid, I'd seen bailiffs knock on neighbours' doors and take their tellies and stereos away. Even though it wasn't my telly that was being taken, I felt this rage for my friends who suddenly didn't have their bikes or their TVs. I knew I had a choice: either walk away from the industry or change it. Driven by my sense of injustice, I saw an opportunity to do enforcement differently by focusing on the people who *wouldn't* pay rather than those who *couldn't*.

I spent a couple of years at that company, where I was so successful, I was promoted to train other staff and oversee the operations. We took part in a prime-time TV series called *Bailiffs*, and as a young, polite and well-dressed member of the staff, I got quite a lot of screen time and became something of a poster boy for the industry. Over the next few years, my level of fame would help open doors and I set up my own company, Wisehill.

On the face of things, my Wisehill business partners weren't that well chosen. The first was one of the biggest debtors I'd ever had to collect from, a larger-than-life character called Frank who drove a bright red Ferrari and was a bit of a geezer. The second was his lawyer, Tony. On the plus side, between them they knew something I didn't: how to run a business. Obviously, I could have learned all the things they knew how to do – incorporate a limited company, set up payroll, file annual accounts – but it would have taken me so much longer. By delegating those tasks to people who knew the ropes, I was freed up to win contracts and pull in the money.

Delegation and coordination, as we have seen time and again in this book, are key dyslexic skills. I used to think this was because dyslexics had no choice but to ask for help with some tasks, but since teaming up with Dr Helen Taylor, I've learned that this skill likely has a different origin: it's because dyslexics are explorers, and view situations at the global level. In order to maintain that breadth and coordinate, we need to delegate to people who can specialise in particular areas. Either way, when you've got a weakness, it makes sense to partner with, or employ, people who have complementary skills.

With Frank and Tony supposedly taking care of the admin, I was free to win contracts. I spent most of those early days wearing a cordless headset, pacing the office and calling up anyone who could give us work. Mostly, these were local authorities trying to collect unpaid fines. It wasn't long before I was generating so much business that I needed to hire staff.

My attitude to hiring then was very similar to how it is now. I don't undertake a rigorous process, but instead tend to go with my gut, another common dyslexic trait. My priority in business is usually to keep moving forward, so if I'm interviewing five people in a day, I'm probably going to hire one of them, even if none of them are perfect. If it doesn't work out, I'm fine with that because I'm quite happy to make a wrong decision. I'll accept 80 per cent quality 100 per cent of the time as that keeps the business moving forward. I'm not a perfectionist.

When Wisehill hit the £1 million turnover mark within a year, I had something of a realisation: of the three directors, I was the only one in the office. Frank and Tony owned two-thirds of the business, but I was doing

98 per cent of the work. Those familiar feelings of injustice meant I couldn't live with the status quo. I offered to value the business at £1 million and buy them out with a payment of £333,333 each. I didn't quite know how I would do it – presumably get a loan that I would repay from revenue – but if they didn't accept the deal, I told them I would walk away.

They didn't even take an hour to discuss my offer: they asked me to leave the building immediately. I couldn't believe it. Really? They *really* wanted me out? They did. So, I packed up a box of my things and walked out of the office, totally blindsided by how suddenly things had changed.

Of course, this was all the motivation I needed to do it all over again. As painful as it was to walk out of Wisehill, deep down I knew that I was the one who had built a million-pound company in under a year, and I knew I could do it again. That night, I sat at my kitchen table and registered the domain name for my new company. Several Wisehill clients and all but one of the staff chose to follow me to my new venture, JBW, a business I would eventually sell for tens of millions.

Before I'd sold JBW, however, I'd had this horrible feeling of 'what am I going to do next?' The prospect of having time on my hands was not just unappealing, it was somehow *impossible* to consider.

I considered getting an MBA as I'd learned so much from participating in business programmes while running JBW. Getting accepted onto an MBA course when I didn't even have a GCSE wasn't going to be straightforward. I contacted the London Business School and asked for an opportunity to present my case to them – you know, this is me, my past success, etc. As part of our discussion, they asked if I had ever been diagnosed with dyslexia. Would I like to take a test to find out? Desperate to be accepted onto their Executive MBA programme, I said yes. That test finally confirmed that I was indeed dyslexic, though LBS never mentioned it again and a few months later I was accepted on their course.

However, such was my inability to do nothing, that by the time term started I had already started my next venture. Hito was a fintech business in the data analytics and behavioural insights space that I'd launched six days after the sale of JBW. When the EMBA classes finally started, my time was almost totally taken up with Hito and I quickly realised I couldn't do both. I decided to focus on building a business rather than learning about the theory of business and reluctantly threw in the towel. It seemed that formal education and me still weren't a good fit.

My brain was getting all the stimulation it needed from growing Hito. My thoughts were in overdrive, planning and problem solving. Now I know more about dyslexia, I understand that hyperactivity is part of it. And the weird thing is, given how hard I was working back then, it wasn't exhausting. Reading a business plan, unlike reading a novel, is fun for me. It absorbs my thoughts so fully that my body gets a chance to relax. Not starting a business would have been way more stressful, and just nine months after I launched Hito I was offered millions to sell it. Obviously, I did the deal.

Within five weeks of selling Hito, I approached the management consultancy Arum, who had represented the buyer of Hito in our negotiations. I liked their people, their brand and the power their business had in the public procurement space. I wanted to own it. Nine weeks later, I completed the transaction and was once again a business owner. Arum was small at the time, just a few million pounds in revenue with hardly any profits, but over the next five years we transformed it. We launched services in Australia, New Zealand and the US, and built a company worth tens of millions of pounds.

With most of my business ventures, I love the early stages when you are resource investigating, putting together teams, designing strategies and developing a plan for how to beat the competition. Which is why, in 2019, a couple of years into building Arum, I appointed a management team and started to think, 'What's next?' In September that year, I launched Just, a technology and data business offering an integrated marketplace of services.

Five months into trading, the world came to a halt when the Covid pandemic struck. By this point, we had spent around a million pounds on the launch and we had to make a decision. Close the business, or keep our heads down and carry on? At a meeting in April 2020, I was asked if we should stop and wait until the pandemic was over to launch. My response was that we would never get an opportunity like it again. When else would all our competitors be sat at home or on the golf course? My answer was that we don't stop, we invest more, we work faster and we carry on. It was a bold decision, but the right one. Just is now one of the most successful businesses in its space.

During the growth stages of Arum and Just, I employed a senior management team to focus on scaling while I launched my venture fund, Love Yellow. Managing the fund is my perfect career. I get to jump from project to project, meaning my hyperactive brain gets all the exercise it needs, and the skills I bring to the table – simplifying the big picture, understanding the numbers and logically being able to see through the bullsh*t – make me good at what I do.

Clearly, dyslexia hasn't stopped me from succeeding – on the contrary, it has almost certainly contributed to my success – but it still causes me problems and anxieties. I rarely write anything longhand, and when I do, my handwriting is deliberately scruffy in the hope that I might disguise my spelling mistakes. Poor spelling is also the main reason I don't really do social media, because I get so annoyed with the small-minded people correcting my mistakes.

Dyslexia involves doing more prep than most people, and I work hard to make sure I'm not ambushed like the time I had to read the story about the praying mantis (as explained in the Introduction). I avoid reading anything out loud that I haven't prepared myself, and these days I simply tell people up front about my dyslexia as I've realised that far from being something to be ashamed of, it's a difference to be proud of.

I do a lot of public speaking and have taught myself tricks for memorising speeches. I will usually get to the room early and make a mental note of things in the venue. I then attach them to a trigger word: for example, a door might remind me to talk about a business exit, or the light fitting will prompt me to talk about innovation. I'm guessing this is something someone who doesn't have dyslexia never needs to worry about. Writing in public still terrifies me almost three decades after I left school. I can't write anything if anyone, including my wife, is looking over my shoulder.

Even at home, dyslexia has an impact. The other day I called out to my wife, Madeleine, how to spell the word 'swimming', and it was my seven-year-old who shouted the answer back! Remarkably, with two dyslexic parents, Amelie and Allegra are excelling at school and do not seem to have inherited it from either of us. Although they are still young.

I sometimes feel a bit useless when I help my kids with their homework, and this could easily get me down. Things got better, however, when I told them about my dyslexia, as that relieved the pressure of having to have all the answers. It also has the added benefit of making them feel brilliant when they know more than me. I hope it gives them an understanding of dyslexia that helps them show more compassion towards their classmates and others.

People knowing about my dyslexia is empowering. I only wish I had been diagnosed earlier, that I had embraced it and told people sooner. Despite everything I've achieved, embracing my dyslexia has been the single most powerful thing I have done in my career. I hope this book inspires others to do the same.

INSIGHTS FROM DR HELEN TAYLOR

Adventuring

Dyslexic people often say they need to 'move to think' and Jamie pacing the office wearing a Bluetooth headset to make calls is a brilliant example of that. It's one reason dyslexic children might have difficulties at school when they have to sit still for much of the day

The connection between the extent we explore in the physical world and the extent we explore in abstract space – our imagination – is deeply ingrained in us. Areas of our brains involved in exploring to find resources in the real world were co-opted over evolutionary time to enable us to explore and find information and ideas in our minds. It's not a coincidence that many professional explorers – Sir Ranulph Fiennes, Sir Peter Scott (creator of the World Wildlife Fund), Ann Bancroft (polar explorer) and Bob Ballard (deep ocean exploration) – are dyslexic. When I learned that Jamie has been a competitor in the Enduro dirt-bike rally across the Sahara, has sailed across the Atlantic and has plans to go into space, I knew he fitted a pattern I see a lot in dyslexic thinkers.

Serial entrepreneurship

This dyslexic drive to explore helps explain why Jamie and many of the others in this book have started multiple businesses. Even as a teenager running his car yard, Jamie was looking for more ways to start new ventures, whether that was hiring out cars or operating taxis. This tendency in dyslexics to seek out new opportunities, and to improve things, is about updating their knowledge rather than exploiting what they already know, i.e. just sticking to one business and incrementally improving it.

CONCLUSION

I started this book with a story of me on a Caribbean island. It seems only fitting to end the book by telling you of my surroundings now. I am sitting in the UK in February, the midpoint of our winter. The days are short, the temperatures cold, and I have been deep into the details of this book for almost exactly a year. I have learned so much, met many wonderful people and read more research than I want to recall. It's not easy when you have dyslexia.

I began this journey wanting to understand the links between dyslexia and successful people and offer readers tips on how to implement dyslexic thinking for their own gain. I hope I have achieved that. During the writing process, however, it's been difficult to ignore the other side of dyslexia. Yes, 40 per cent of self-made millionaires are dyslexic, but so are 50 per cent of prisoners. It's a statistic that's just as important, and one we need to do more to change.

It has been a challenge to find a reason why, historically, we have assumed people who learn differently have a disability at all. Dr Helen Taylor explained that, in terms of human existence, writing is a relatively new technology and in a pre-literate age, the people who now struggle with reading and writing would not have been described as deficient in any way. But now that education is based around the written word, we realise we have devised a learning system that is not right for 15 per cent of the population.

Fifteen per cent of the global population equates to over a billion people. It is unfathomable to me that no one is talking about reimagining our education systems to make them work for everyone. Think of the transformation that would come from engaging every young mind in study. Think of the impact on the economy. Think of the effect on prison statistics. Think of the lives that would be transformed. With technology and Artificial Intelligence (AI) forecast to be increasingly used in education, this is not an unachievable ambition.

Until governments across the globe redesign systems to include dyslexic thinkers, it is down to us to accept the challenge. If we do, we can increase the number of people with dyslexia who reach their full potential. We must find practical steps to improve effective educational intervention *and* change people's perceptions about dyslexia.

The International Dyslexia Association believes that dyslexic people deserve identification and intervention as early as possible. This is supported by most of the public, who agree with the statement: 'Children can, over time, be taught to compensate for learning disabilities with early diagnosis and proper instruction.'* Unfortunately, as with Harry and Terry, who we met in the Introduction, early identification is not the norm. Parental misconceptions are

---

*   https://dyslexiaida.org/ida-lda-whitepaper

sometimes to blame, because parents sometimes think – or maybe hope – that signs of learning difficulties are something young children will outgrow. We hear time and again that schools are still ill-equipped to identify dyslexia early on. Training for both parents and teachers is a path to early intervention, and while some countries around the world are supplying funding for such training, many still need to do so. That means charities are often left to step in where governments are failing.

A great example is Made By Dyslexia (madebydyslexia. org), the charity we heard about in Chapter 13, which offers both teachers and parents FREE tools that specifically focus on the identification of dyslexia. We know that the earlier interventions are started, the better the educational outcomes, so I encourage governments to promote, rather than ignore, these useful resources. We need to see a paradigm shift in both research and education in how we understand and nurture people with this more exploratory way of learning.

Data collected by the National Center for Learning Disabilities in 2014 found that 43 per cent of respondents of a survey believed that learning difficulties are associated with low IQ. We must change this perception, and an excellent place to start is with the facts:

- Dyslexia is neurobiological in origin and affects how a person's brain processes information, resulting in an unexpected underachievement in the human-made technologies of reading, writing and maths.

- Dyslexia is not an indication of intelligence.

- 40 per cent of self-made millionaires are known to be dyslexic, as are 35 per cent of entrepreneurs.

- People with dyslexia can attain the same academic achievements as those without when the appropriate educational interventions and other support are provided to them.

Dyslexia is a different way of thinking that requires a different learning approach. The untapped potential of people with dyslexia is a tragedy for the individual that also has a profound impact on society. Dyslexics often report anxiety about school and refuse to go, sometimes dropping out of education entirely. Those who persevere frequently experience extreme difficulties and stress and never reach their full potential. They may receive lower levels of qualifications and as a result are more often unemployed than those without dyslexia, despite comparable levels of intelligence. Even if they achieve higher levels of qualifications, it is often at the expense of their health and self-esteem.

If we change our education system, how many of the dyslexics who end up in prison might feature among lists of high achievers like Charles Schwab, Walt Disney, Whoopi Goldberg and Steven Spielberg?

The impact of these changes on individuals is immeasurable, but we can also attempt to calculate the at the impact it would have on the global economy. The UCSF Dyslexia Center and the Boston Consulting Group published a White Paper in July 2020, titled *The Economic Impact of Dyslexia on California*. They estimated the cost to California of failing dyslexics was approximately $12 billion in 2020 and over the next sixty years it would rise to $1 trillion. *Trillion.* Just in California. Now imagine what the impact would be globally. If you took California's share of GDP, which was 3.7 per cent in 2020, and applied it to the estimated global population of roughly 7.8 billion in the same year, the potential global impact was $455 billion. Cumulatively, that could reach a staggering $40 trillion over the same sixty-year period.

By reaching the end of this book, you have made your own positive contribution to changing the perceptions of dyslexia. For those of you with dyslexia, I hope the book and the brilliant stories motivate you to use your superpowers to succeed. For those of you without dyslexia, I hope you have collected some useful dyslexic thinking tips and that they serve you well.

Jamie Waller

ACKNOWLEDGEMENTS

I would like to thank several people who made this book possible:

Sir Richard Branson for planting the seed.

The brilliant contributors who through their transparency and vulnerability will help change the narrative of dyslexia: Cliff Weitzman, Sir Charles Dunstone, Kelly Hoppen, Wilfred Emmanuel-Jones, Edward Keelan, Theo Paphitis, Paul Orfalea, Joseph Rapaport, Duncan Bannatyne, Harry Warren, Matt Kennedy, Philli Armitage-Mattin, Nigel Cabourn, Richard White, Kate Griggs and Dr Helen Taylor.

Jo Monroe and Michael Heppell for their brilliant ideas and help with writing.

And my family for affording me the time to travel the world performing interviews and work endless nights from the kitchen table at our home, in Henley-on-Thames, UK.